ESDRA'S
THREE-HEADED
EAGLE

Surely the Lord God does nothing, unless He reveals
His secret to His servants the prophets.
(Amos 3:7)

Books by Best-Selling Author James Harman

The Final Countdown[1]
The Open Door[1]
Salvation of the Soul[1]
Daniel's Prophecies Unsealed[1,2]
Come Away My Beloved
Calling All Overcomers
Overcomers' Guide to the Kingdom
The Kingdom
The Coming Spiritual Earthquake[1]
The Blessed Hope

Books by Award Winning Author Dr. Christian Widener

Witnessing The End
The Temple Revealed[3]

1) Amazon #1 New Release Best Seller.
2) Amazon Top 10 Best Selling Book under Christian Old Testament Commentaries from 2018 to 2024.
3) First Place 2022 Christian Indie Award Winner that showed the true location of the Jewish Temple. Josh McDowell wrote in the foreword to *The Temple Revealed*: "The implications of his findings are nothing short of world-changing."

ESDRA'S THREE-HEADED EAGLE

James T. Harman

Prophecy
Countdown
Publications

Esdra's Three-Headed Eagle

ISBN: 978-1-7332995-8-9 (Paperback)
ISBN: 978-1-7332995-9-6 (eBook)

Dedication

After the second edition of this series
Was published in 2023,
Our beautiful daughter Jennifer
Went to be with the Lord.
We are confident that
She is now free from all pain
And rejoicing with
Our Wonderful Saviour!

This third and final edition
Is also lovingly dedicated
To Jennifer who was such an
Inspiration to all who knew her!

To learn more about her incredible life
And to watch her Celebration of Life
Please visit her website:
www.ThreeFeetDeep.com

Is God a Date Setter?

- God set a date for the flood and revealed it to righteous Noah (Genesis 7:11).
- God set a date for the destruction of Sodom and revealed it to Abraham and Lot (Genesis 18, 19).
- God set a date for Isaac to be born and told it to Sarah and Abraham (Genesis 17:21).
- God set a date for Israel to come out of Egypt and revealed it centuries before he instructed Moses to do so (Genesis 15:13; Gal 3:14-17; Exodus 12:40).
- God set a date for the cattle of Egypt to die and told Moses and Pharaoh (Exodus 12:40).
- God set a date for the defeat of Moab and revealed it to Isaiah earlier (Isaiah 16:14).
- God set a date for the end of the Babylonian captivity and revealed it to Jeremiah decades in advance (Jeremiah 25:11).
- God set a date for the fall of Babylon and told it to Jeremiah and revealed it to Daniel (Jer 27:4-7; Daniel 5:25-30).
- God set a date for the first coming of Jesus Christ and told it to Daniel, Mary, Joseph, and Simeon in advance (Daniel 9; Mat 1:18-25; Luke 2:26-32).

Surely the Lord God does nothing, unless He reveals
His secret to His servants the prophets.
(Amos 3:7 – NKJV)

"When the Spirit of truth comes, he will guide you into all
truth. He will not speak on his own but will tell you what
he has heard. He will tell you about the future.
(John 16:13 – NLT)

Prologue

On May 19, 2023, my beautiful daughter Jennifer turned 41 and she was rushed to the hospital where she was placed on a ventilator. She spent the next 68 days fighting to recover from various medical issues relating to her quadriplegia. I spent many of those days in her room, encouraging her and praying for her recovery. Much of the time she would be sleeping and I utilized this time to study a new finding in the 11th and 12th chapters of the book of 2 Esdras.

A lady who lives in central Florida named Barbara Schoble-Legee discovered that this little-known book contains a remarkable prophecy covering the Presidents of the United States starting with Herbert Hoover down to Barack Obama. In her book, she explains where the book of 2 Esdras shows that President Biden's term of office will be shorter than President Trump's. Anyone following the news would probably agree that her prediction is not that far-fetched. What is interesting, however, is what I believe the book of 2 Esdras predicts after he is no longer in office. That is the subject of this book.

Those who are familiar with my latest book: *The Final Countdown* know that I believe that the Antichrist may make his appearance sometime during 2024. This view is predicated on the belief that God foreknew and ordained a Second Fulfillment to the prophecy regarding the Seventy Weeks of Daniel. This brand new understanding is based upon Dr. Christian Widener's discovery that the Second Fulfillment of Daniel's prophecy may have begun with Sultan Suleiman's decree in 1537. Moving forward 70 weeks (490 years) brings us to the Second Coming of Christ in 2027. If his interpretation is correct, then it would mean that the final 3 ½ years of *Great Tribulation* would need to begin sometime this year (please see Chart at the end of this Prologue).

Because Jennifer recently went to be with the Lord, I have been delayed in publishing this book. I believe God wants this important material available to the body of Christ because, if this analysis is correct, the Antichrist is about to make his appearance before Biden's successor is allowed in office.

Daniel's Prophecies Unsealed was our first book on Daniel where we describe how the first two beasts in Daniel 7, have already appeared with the lion (England) and the bear (Russia). The third beast is described as a leopard and we believe that it is about to make its entrance on the world scene. This third beast will be comprised of the 5 nations that are listed in Psalm 83: Egypt, Syria, Iraq, Jordan, and Saudia Arabia. Interestingly, the two other people groups that are included in Psalm 83 are Philistia (Gaza) and Tyre (Lebanon). This Psalm tells us the purpose of their conspiracy against Israel: *4) They have said, 'Come, and let us cut them off from being a nation, That the name of Israel may be remembered no more. 5) For they have consulted together with one consent; They form a confederacy against You...*(Psalm 83:4-5 – NKJV)

The recent war in Gaza is most likely a precursor to what they are planning in order to remove Israel from the map. If our analysis of the hidden prophecy in 2 Esdras outlined in this book is correct, we will probably witness the fulfillment of Daniel's prophecy very soon.

This means that some major crisis will occur in the Middle East, which will force Daniel's third beast to arise and be given dominion. The forming of this Arab coalition will then be the catalyst for the final fourth beast, along with the Antichrist, to also appear.

> *15) Therefore when you see the abomination of desolation, spoken of by Daniel the prophet, **standing in the holy place...21) For then there will be great tribulation**, such as has not been seen since the beginning of the world until this time, no, nor ever shall be.* (Matthew 24:15, 21 – NKJV)

The appearance of the Antichrist on the Temple Mount will be the start of the final 3 ½ years of *Great Tribulation* before Jesus returns at His Second Coming. Now is the time to prepare ourselves and to help others prepare. Jesus does provide a way of escape for those blameless believers (2 Peter 3:14) who are earnestly praying as He taught us to pray:

*36) Watch ye therefore, and pray always, that ye may be **accounted worthy to escape** all these things that shall come to pass, and to stand before the Son of man.* (Luke 21:36)

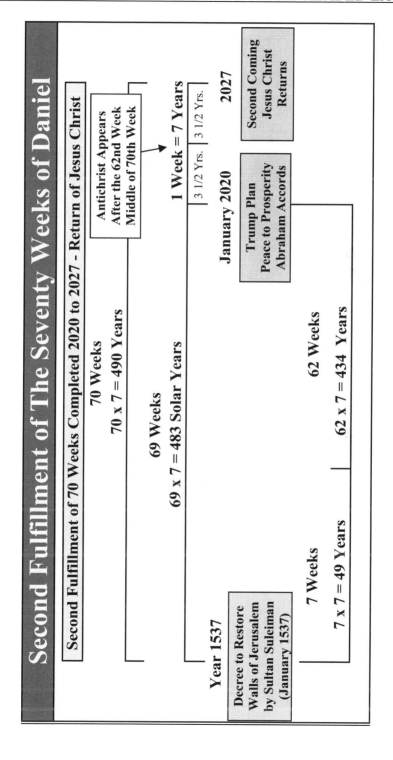

THE WATCHMAN

(Pastors, Teachers, Evangelists, and Saints)
Ezekiel the Watchman for Israel
Again the word of the LORD came to me, saying,

2 "Son of man, speak to your people and tell them: 'Suppose I bring the sword against a land, and the people of that land choose a man from among them, appointing him as their watchman, 3 and he sees the sword coming against that land and blows the ram's horn to warn the people.

4 Then if anyone hears the sound of the horn but fails to heed the warning, and the sword comes and takes him away, his blood will be on his own head. 5 Since he heard the sound of the horn but failed to heed the warning, his blood will be on his own head. If he had heeded the warning, he would have saved his life.

6 But if the watchman sees the sword coming and fails to blow the horn to warn the people, and the sword comes and takes away a life, then that one will be taken away in his iniquity, but I will hold the watchman accountable" (Ezekiel 33:2-6 – BSB).

Table of Contents

3) The voice of one crying in the wilderness:
"Prepare the way of the Lord;
Make straight in the desert
A highway for our God.
4) Every valley shall be exalted
And every mountain and hill brought low;
The crooked places shall be made straight
And the rough places smooth;
5) The glory of the Lord shall be revealed,
And all flesh shall see it together;
For the mouth of the Lord has spoken."
(Isaiah 40:3-5 – NKJV)

John the Baptist Prepares the Way
In those days John the Baptist came preaching
in the wilderness of Judea, and saying,
"Repent for the kingdom of heaven is at hand!"
For this is he who was spoken of by the prophet Isaiah…
(Matthew 3:1-3 – NKJV)

Foreward
MAYDAY — MAYDAY --- MAYDAY – RED ALERT

This book was not something that I ever wanted to write. Who would ever desire to write a message that says that time is almost up? Or to tell people that this may be the last chance you have to prepare to meet Jesus!

Following in the footsteps of Edgar Wisenant is not something anyone would aspire to. For those who are not familiar with Edgar Wisenant, he was the scientist who predicted the Lord would return in 1988.

Despite Edgar's incorrect prediction, his writings got me interested in prophecy and I have been a diligent student of the prophetic Word ever since. I have been labeled as a date setter before, but my intentions have never been to set an exact date for the Lord's return.

As outlined in the Prologue, the main thesis of this book is that the Second Coming of Christ should take place in 2027. This is based upon Dr. Christian Widener's discovery of the decree made by Sultan Suleiman in 1537 as outlined in *The Final Countdown*. Since he restored Jerusalem between the years 1537 to 1541, it may be possible that the start date for the initial decree could be off by a year or so. This would mean that 2020 was not the beginning of the final 7 years and that 2024 could be when the Second Fulfillment of Daniel's Seventy Weeks should begin. This would then place the Second Coming around 2031 with the final 3 ½ years beginning in 2028.

The above analysis could be correct, however, when I discovered the prophecy in 2 Esdras it changed my perspective on everything. What you are about to read in this booklet shows that 2024 really could be the year for the Antichrist to make his appearance. This is based upon my interpretation of this ancient prophecy, which has been hidden in a book that was removed from our Bibles in 1885. If my understanding of this is not correct, then I ask for you to please forgive me.

Jim Harman
Prophecy Countdown Publications

Note: Why Foreward vs. Foreword? Timothy Schwab coined this change in his book: *2 Esdras – The Hidden Book of Prophecy* where he stated:

> "…wanted something more for the opening words that sets the tone appropriately…employing a sort of double entendre in using the word Foreward reviving an Old English word far more significant. Foreward means to keep guard, vanguard, protect, tend, etc…This work also strives to move a people forward out of the Dark Ages which still persist. For this book, that is the title chosen very appropriately in raising the curtain on this work."[1]

According to Wikipedia, the term Mayday originated as an emergency procedure word used internationally as a distress signal.

It is used to signal a life-threatening emergency primarily by aviators and mariners, but in some countries, local organizations such as firefighters, police forces, and transportation organizations also use the term. The standard convention requires the word to be repeated three times in a row during the initial emergency declaration, i.e.: **"Mayday mayday mayday."**

There may be some people who will say that the motive behind this booklet is to make money. We can assure these people that any profit from this book will be given to a charity such as Joni and Friends or the Jesus Film Project (two of Jennifer's favorite charities).

---

1) Timothy Schwab, 2 Esdras: The Hidden Book of Prophecy (The Levite Bible 2021): 2

Preface

2 Timothy 2:15 (KJV) admonishes us: *Study to shew thyself approved unto God, a workman that needeth not be ashamed, rightly dividing the word of truth.* He goes on to say in 2 Timothy 3:16-17 (NKJV): *All scripture is given by inspiration of God, and is profitable for doctrine, for reproof, for correction, for instruction in righteousness,17) that the man of God may be complete, thoroughly equipped for every good work.*

Many Christians immediately scoff whenever someone discusses a possible time for Christ's return. This attitude breaks the Lord's heart because He wants His Bride to be watching and He wants us all to remain teachable and humble under His Word.

The purpose of this booklet is to alert everyone as to the lateness of the hour....To the Bride of Christ to get her wedding garments made ready (Revelation 19:7-9) and made spotless (Ephesians 5:27) and to the lost sinners of the world to turn to Jesus while there is still time.

Habakkuk 2:3 (NIV) says: *For the revelation awaits **an appointed time**; it speaks of the end and will not prove false. Though it linger, wait for it; **it will certainly come** and will not delay.*

The Lord has appointed a time when He plans to bring an end to all things. Time is quickly running out, the ***appointed time*** is here.

God wants us to be aware of the time He will return; His Second Coming is one of the central doctrines of His Word. He told us we should be watching, and He gave many wonderful clues to those who will diligently study His Word. The words of the Prophet Daniel are very timely for the days we are living in:

> *9) "Go on your way, Daniel," he replied, "for the words are closed up and sealed **until the time of the end**. 10) Many will be **purified**, made **spotless**, and **refined**, but the wicked will continue to act wickedly. None of the wicked will understand, but the wise will understand* (Daniel 12:9-10 – BSB).

The message in this booklet is that Jesus is returning much sooner than most people think. If you have not been watching, begin "watching" today before it is too late!

Could this book be another false alarm? Yes, it is possible. I could have misinterpreted some things, however, I believe that God has called me to be a watchman for such a time as this. If I am wrong, then I humbly apologize, but I believe that He wants me to sound the alarm.

One of the reasons for this message could be as the Apostle John so aptly put it:

> *Everyone who has this hope (of Christ's return) in him **purifies** himself, just as He is **pure*** (1 John 3:3).

The message of Christ's soon return will purify the hearts of those who are His children. It is time for all of us to purify our hearts and to be properly prepared when Jesus returns for us.

Chapter 1

2nd Esdras

Should Esdras Be In Your Bible?

Many people don't realize that the book of 2 Esdras was included in the King James Bible of 1611. The books of the Apocrypha were included in the original King James Version but were removed in 1885 when the Revised Version was created.

Even before the King James Bible, the Geneva Bible of 1560 included the book of 2 Esdras. This was the Bible of the Protestant Reformation and it was the Bible that the Pilgrims brought with them on their voyage to America on the Mayflower.

2 Esdras Quoted by Jesus

Also, many people are not aware that the book of 2 Esdras was actually quoted by Jesus. One clear example can be found in the first chapter of 2 Esdras:

> 30) I gathered you *as a hen gathers her chicks under her wings*, But now, what shall I do to you? I will cast you out from my presence…32) I sent you my servants the prophets, but you have taken and killed them and torn their bodies in pieces…33) "Thus says the Lord Almighty: *Your house is desolate*; I will drive you out as the wind drives straw;
> (2 Esdras 1:30, 32, 33 – NRSV)

And now compare this to what Jesus said as recorded in Matthew:

> 37) O Jerusalem, Jerusalem, the one who kills the prophets and stones those who are sent to her! How often I wanted to gather your children together, *as a hen gathers her chicks under her wings*, but you were not willing! 38) See! *Your house is left to you desolate*;
> (Matthew 23:37-38 – NKJV)

We find it very interesting that our Lord actually quoted from the book of 2 Esdras. The controversy revolves around whether Jesus quoted from 2 Esdras or if 2 Esdras was written after Jesus lived and 2 Esdras was written after His death.

While researching this debate we discovered an excellent book entitled: *2 Esdras – The Hidden Book of Prophecy*, which was written by Timothy Schwab and Anna Zamoranos. They provide a very strong case that 2 Esdras was not written in 70-218 AD, as advocated by current scholars. Their analysis helps lend credence to the argument that 2 Esdras may have been written around 400 BC by the Prophet Ezra himself or perhaps his scribe.

This understanding can also be seen in another prophecy recorded in the seventh chapter of 2 Esdras:

> 26) For indeed the time will come, when the signs that I have foretold to you will come to pass, that the city [New Jerusalem] that now is not shall appear, and the land that now is hidden shall be disclosed…28) For my *son the Messiah* shall be revealed with those who are with him, and those who remain shall rejoice [within – KJV] *four hundred years.* 29) *After those years my son the Messiah shall die*… (2 Esdras 7:26, 28-29 – NRSV)

Ezra may have written the above messianic prophecy around the year 400 BC. It predicts that Jesus would come after four hundred years and then He would die. If Ezra was the author it adds credibility to the fact that 2 Esdras should be part of our inspired scripture.

2 Esdras Read By Early Disciples

What if you were told that the Bible records the name of an early disciple who probably read the book of 2 Esdras? Wouldn't that give more credence to the fact that it should be in our Bibles today?

One of the shortest books in the New Testament is the letter by the Apostle Paul to Philemon. Many Christians have probably never heard of it before but it is located between Titus and the Book of Hebrews.

I can remember reading this beautiful book when I first came to Christ because of the wonderful way the Apostle Paul asks for Onesimus to be treated.

Philemon was a Christian slave owner and Onesimus was one of his slaves who had run away but subsequently converted to Christ by Paul. Paul pleads that his new convert be considered as a brother in Christ.

> 17) If then you count me as a partner, receive him [Onesimus] as you would me. 18) But if he has wronged you or owes anything, put that on my account. 19) I Paul, am writing with my own hand. I will repay – not to mention to you that you owe me even your own self besides. 20) Yes, brother, let me have joy from you in the Lord; refresh my heart in the Lord (Philemon 17-20 – NKJV).

Paul had also previously converted Philemon and he now tells him he will take on any debt that Onesimus owes him. What a magnificent way to describe how we should treat fellow believers.

(Saint) Melito of Sardis
One of the early church fathers was a man by the name of (Saint) Melito of Sardis who died in 180 AD. Jerome quotes Melito who was held in high regard, particularly for his work on developing the first Canon of the Old Testament. He was known to be a prolific writer, but unfortunately, very few fragments of his writing remain.

Providentially we do have his writing to Onesimus:

> "Melito to his brother Onesimus, greeting:
>
> Prompted by your regard for the Word, you have often expressed a wish to have some extracts made from the Law and the Prophets concerning the Savior, I accordingly proceeded to the East, and went to the very spot where these things were preached and took place. Having made myself <u>accurately</u> acquainted with the books of the Old Testament, I have set them down below, and herewith send you the list.

…Their names are as follows: The five books of Moses–(Genesis, Exodus, Leviticus, Numbers, Deuteronomy). Joshua son of Nun., Judges, Ruth, the four books of Kings, the two of Chronicles, the Psalms of David, the Proverbs of Solomon, also called Wisdom. Ecclesiastes, the Song of Songs, Job, the prophets Isaiah and Jeremiah, the twelve [minor prophets] contained in a single book. **Daniel, Ezekiel, Esdras**, from these I have made my extracts, dividing them into **six books**."[1]

At the very end of his list, he mentions: Daniel, Ezekiel, and Esdras. He then states that from these three names mentioned, he had divided them into six books:

Where Esdras = [Ezra, Nehemiah, 1 Esdras & 2 Esdras] Therefore: The 6 books = Daniel, Ezekiel, Ezra, Nehemiah, 1 Esdras, & 2 Esdras.

This would mean that he considered 1 Esdras and 2 Esdras to be two of the 6 books included in his list given to Onesimus.

From this, we have learned that Onesimus had a high regard for the Word of God and a desire to learn more about the Old Testament. Based upon Sanit Melito's compilation, the books named Esdras consisted of four books, which would include 1 Esdras and 2 Esdras. This provides compelling evidence that 2 Esdras was probably read by Onesimus, one of the Apostle Paul's converts.

Should Esdras be in your Bible?
It appears that the two books of Esdras were included in the Bible from the time of the Apostle Paul. We have also seen that the Pilgrims read the book of 2 Esdras in their Geneva Bibles of 1560. When the King James Bible was authorized in 1611 the book of 2 Esdras was also included. It wasn't until 1885 that these books were removed from our Bibles.

Based upon this summary it appears the book of 2 Esdras should be included in our Bibles of today.

---

1) David W. Bercot, Editor, *A Dictionary of Early Christian Beliefs* (Hendrickson Publishers 2019): 84-85.

Chapter 2

Chapters 11 and 12 of 2nd Esdras

Prophetic Message for USA

The complete text for Chapters 11 and 12 of 2nd Esdras is included in Appendix 2 (New Revised Standard version) and Appendix 3 (Anchor Bible version). You may want to read either of these before you begin this chapter. While this is not absolutely necessary, it will give you a flavor for these important chapters.

When we wrote the first edition of **Daniel's Prophecies Unsealed** back in 2018, we never anticipated we would produce two more. We quoted the following from the book of 2 Esdras to show why America is the 4th beast in Daniel 7:

> …1) I had a dream I saw <u>rising from the sea</u> an <u>eagle</u>…2) I saw it spread its wings <u>over the whole</u> <u>earth</u>…5) and it <u>reigned over the earth</u> and over those who inhabit it…6) all things under heaven were subjected to it, and no one spoke against it–not a single creature…on the earth. (2 Esdras 11:1, 2, 5, & 6 – NRSV)

> 10) He said to me, "This is the <u>interpretation of this</u> <u>vision</u> that you have seen: 11) the <u>eagle</u> that you saw coming up from the sea is the <u>fourth kingdom</u> that appeared in a <u>vision</u> to your brother <u>Daniel</u>. (2 Esdras 12:10-11 – NRSV)

This prophecy clearly reveals that the United States of America, whose national symbol is the Eagle, relates to the description of the vision that was given to the Prophet Daniel.

One thing that is important to note is how the 12th chapter of 2 Edras usually provides an interpretation of what was given in chapter 11. This is a key when trying to understand how the prophecy is expected to play out.

If you have read either of the appendixes, you realize that Ezra speaks a great deal about wings and heads rising, ruling, and disappearing. Because we know that these prophecies are about America we should look into our past rulers (presidents) to see where to begin and to help us understand how 2 Esdras relates to where we are in time.

Franklin Delano Roosevelt (FDR)

In order to find where FDR may be mentioned in 2 Esdras we need to find a place where it mentions a president who was in office for a long period of time.

> 12 As I watched, <u>one wing</u> on the right side rose up, and it reigned over all the earth. 13 And after a time its reign came to an end, and it disappeared, so that even its place was no longer visible. Then the <u>next wing</u> rose up and reigned, ***and it continued to reign a long time***. 14 While it was reigning its end came also, so that it disappeared like the first. 15 And a voice sounded, saying to it, 16 ***"Listen to me, you who have ruled the earth all this time;*** I announce this to you before you disappear. ***17 After you no one shall rule as long as you have ruled, not even half as long***."
> (2 Esdras 11:13-17 – NRSV)

FDR was in office from 1933 to 1945 for a period of over 12 years. Because he had been elected to four terms in office, congress passed the 22nd Amendment, which prohibits all future Presidents from serving more than two terms. This ensures verse 17 in the above prophecy will be fulfilled because all presidents after FDR are limited to 8 years in office.

We continue with Ezra's narrative:

> 18 Then the <u>third wing</u> raised itself up, and held the rule as the earlier ones had done, and it also disappeared. 19 And so it went with all the wings; they wielded power one after another and then were never seen again. 20 I kept looking, and in due time the wings that followed also rose up on the right side, in order to rule. There were some of them that ruled, yet disappeared suddenly; 21 and ***others of them rose up, but did not hold the rule***.

22 And after this I looked and saw that *the twelve wings and the two little wings had disappeared*, 23 and nothing remained on the eagle's body except the three heads that were at rest and six little wings.

Prophecy – History Written In Advance
Ezra's prophetic timeline for the United States of America begins in 2 Esdras 11:12, with "one wing on the right side." It is followed by the second wing in verse 13, which we have determined to be FDR. Each wing represents an American President and the prophecy continues as each one reigns for a period and is then followed by another. This continues until verse 22 after 14 wings have served their term in office (12 regular wings and 2 little wings). The little wings refer to the Presidents whose term in office was cut short (John F. Kennedy who was assassinated and Richard Nixon who was impeached).

Since we know FDR was the second wing in Esdras prophecy, the first wing would have been Herbert Hoover who was the 31st President of the United States. The succession of these 14 wings can be summarized as follows:

Wing	**President**	**Term in Office**	
1	Herbert Hoover	1929-1933	
2	Franklin D. Roosevelt	1933-1945	
3	Harry S. Truman	1945-1953	
4	Dwight D. Eisenhower	1953-1961	
5	John F. Kennedy	1961-1963	Short
6	Lyndon B. Johnson	1963-1969	
7	Richard M. Nixon	1969-1974	Short
8	Gerald R. Ford	1974-1977	
9	Jimmy Carter	1977-1981	
10	Ronald Reagen	1981-1989	
11	George H.W. Bush	1989-1993	
12	Bill Clinton	1993-2001	
13	George W. Bush	2001-2009	
14	Barack Obama	2009-2017	

Total = 88 Years

The prophecy after the first 14 Presidents continues with 8 wings who will reign for a shorter period of time that will pass by swiftly as predicted in 2 Esdras 12:19-20:

> 19 As for your seeing *eight little wings* clinging to its wings, this is the <u>interpretation:</u> 20 *Eight kings shall arise in it, whose times shall be short and their years swift*; (2 Esdras 12:19-20)

This means that the period of time for the 8 Presidents after Barack Obama will be shorter and will go by more quickly. Notice that verses 19 and 20 (from chapter 12) are an interpretation of what was told in chapter 11. This is where the prophecy becomes more difficult to decipher.

22) And after this, I looked and saw the twelve wings and the two little wings had disappeared 23) and nothing remained on the eagle's body except the *three heads* that were at rest and the **six** little wings.

24) As I kept looking I saw that **two** little wings[a&5] **separated** from the **six** and remained under the head that was on the right side; but **four** remained in their place (2 Esdras 11:22-24).

The *three heads* are different from the wings and they will be discussed a little later. Notice that after the 14 wings (12 + 2) disappeared there were 6 little wings in verse 23. Then in verse 24, 2 little wings separated from the others. Per the interpretation in 2 Esdras 12:19-20, we are told that there are 8 little wings in total – the 6 little wings in 2 Esdras 11:23 and the 2 little wings in 2 Esdras 11:24 that separated from the others giving us a total of 8 little wings.

Presidents After Barack Obama
25) Then I saw that these little wings (H. Clinton and T. Kane)[b] *planned* to set themselves up and hold the rule.
26) As I kept looking, one was set up (Trump), but suddenly disappeared; 27) a second also, (Biden) and this disappeared more quickly than the first [less than 4-year term] (2 Esdras 11:25-27).

Clinton and Kane (2 wings) lost to Trump (1 wing) and he then lost to Biden (1 wing) – A total of 4 wings mentioned up to this point.

Footnotes to Chapter 2

a) 2 Esdras 11:24 is interpreted in 2 Esdras 12:29: *"It is these (two little wings) whom the Most High has kept for the eagle's end."* This is the time of the **great tribulation**.

5   2 Esdras 12:19-21: *"19) As for your seeing **eight little wings** clinging to its wings, this is the interpretation: 20) **Eight kings** shall arise in it, whose time shall be short and their years swift; 21) **two** of them shall perish when the middle of its time draws near;* (President and VP Candidates to perish in the very middle of the Seven year period between 2020 and 2027) *and **four** shall be kept for the time when its end approaches* (Hillary Clinton, Tim Kane, Donald Trump, and Joe Biden), *but **two** shall be kept until the end* (Obama? and Clinton?)."

[2 Esdras 12:29: *"It is these (two little wings) whom the Most High has kept for the eagle's end."*]

The **eight little wings** that are described here represent the eight **"rival wings,"** mentioned in 2 Esdras 11:11. This helps explain how there are two wings that **separated** from the six, making a total of **eight wings** (interpreted as **kings**):

b   Verse 23 ends with three heads and six little wings. Verse 24 shows that two of these wings who did not rule separated from the six (see footnote #5). Verse 25 then introduces **two** wings who were *planning* to set themselves up to run for president and vice president after Obama's term ended. We know these two people were Hillary Clinton and Tim Kane who ran for office in 2016 (planned to hold the rule) but did not rule.

SUMMARY OF THE 8 LITTLE WINGS

Wings	Person	Verses	Time Period
2	Clinton and Kane	11:25	2016
1	Trump	11:26	2016-2020
1	Biden	11:27	2020-2024
4	(*Kept for when time approaches*)		
2	President & VP[c]	11:28-30	2024
2	2 – *Kept for the End*	12:29	2024-2027
8			Total = 12 Years

The following verse explains the chart on the previous page:

> 21 ***two of them*** **shall perish when the middle of its time draws near**, and ***four shall be kept*** **for the time when its end approaches**, but ***two shall be kept*** **until the end.** (2 Esdras 12:21 – NRSV)

The two who perish when the middle of the time draws near are the two candidates who are planning to rule together in 11:28-30 below. The middle of the time would be in the very middle of the Seven year period between 2020 and 2027, which would be in 2024.

2024 Campaign for President

At this point in our time frame, the prophecy states that Biden's term will be shorter than Trump's (11:27). Since Trump was in office for the full four years, this would mean Biden's term will be shortened. How and when this occurs is not specified. The prophecy continues:

28) While I continued to look the **two** that remained (President Candidate and VP Candidate)[c] were *planning* between themselves to **reign together**; 29) and while they were *planning*, one of the **heads** that were at rest (the one that was in the middle)[2] suddenly **awoke**; [Does God raise the Antichrist from the grave?] it was greater than the other *two heads* [see footnote #3]

30) And I saw how it **allied** the *two heads*[3] with itself, 31) and how the head turned with those that were with it and ***devoured*** the two little wings (President and VP Candidates)[c] that were *planning* to reign.

32) Moreover this head gained control of the whole earth, and with much oppression dominated its inhabitants; it had greater power over the world than all the wings that had gone before.

33) After this I looked again and saw the head in the middle suddenly disappear, just as the wings had done. 34) But the two heads remained[4] (Antichrist and False Prophet), which in like manner ruled over the earth and its inhabitants. (2 Esdras 11:28-34)

> *Note: The* **speculations** *in this analysis are not meant to assert the dogmatic identities of the various leaders involved.* **We do not know** *for sure who God will use to orchestrate His final plan, but this little-known book could provide us with some important clues.*

Footnotes to Chapter 2

1) 2 Esdras 12:22-25: *"22) As for your seeing **three heads** at rest, this is the interpretation: 23) In its last days the Most High will **raise up three _kings_**, and they shall renew many things in it, and **shall rule the earth** 24) and its inhabitants more oppressively than all who were before them. Therefore they are called the **heads of the eagle** because it is they who shall sum up his wickedness and **perform his last actions**.*

2) The **head in the middle** was greater than the others and stands for the **Antichrist**, whom God raises up for the final 3 ½ years.

3) Verses 33-34, describe the other **two heads**: **Prince Charles**** is the leader of the Lion (England), which is the 1st beast in Daniel 7:4, he could become one of the **three heads** of the eagle in Esdras 11:23. The 4th beast in Daniel 7:7, which will be led by the **Antichrist** (little horn), will also be **allied** with the **False Prophet**, who is another of the three heads.

   ** Some believe one of the 3 heads could be **Barack Obama**.

4) The two heads that remained in 2 Esdras 11:34 are explained in 2 Esdras 12:26-27: *"26) As for your seeing that the large head disappeared, one of the kings shall die in his bed* (**Prince Charles or Obama**), *but in agonies. 27) But as for the two who remained* (**Antichrist** and the **False Prophet**), *the sword shall devour them."* (This will take place at the very end of the **great tribulation** period as described in Revelation 19:20-21).

The Three Heads

Esdra's **three heads** begin their activity when the two wings in Esdras 11:28-29 begin their "**_planning_** *between themselves* **to reign together.**" These two wings appear right after Biden, so we are assuming they represent the Presidential and Vice Presidential candidates[c]. We do not know for certain who they are.

As described in the above footnotes these three heads are three kings who will rule the earth at the very end (3 ½ years of Great Tribulation). The head in the middle (2 Esdras 11:29) awakes suddenly and he is described as greater than the other two heads. We are assuming this head represents the Antichrist whom God allows to arise at this time. The identity of the other two heads is purely speculative by this author.

Many people believe Prince Charles is the Antichrist, but he could be one of the three heads in Esdras's prophecy because he would be the leader of the 1st beast (England) in Daniel's prophecy (Daniel 7:4). The other head would most likely be the False Prophet because he will rule with the Antichrist during the final 3 ½ years of Great Tribulation.

The actual identity of the three heads is speculative, however, the startling message 2 Esdras provides is astounding! These three heads are about to take control of the whole world! This prophecy tells us one of their first actions is to *devour* the two people who are planning to reign for our country. This is quite disconcerting for those who love the United States of America. The comment I made in the Epilogue of our first edition of this book in 2018 applies even more so today:

> Living in the United States of America, I sincerely hope that some of the interpretations given in this book on Daniel's visions are wrong. We love our country and are deeply saddened to see the direction it has taken. We were once a great nation that was greatly blessed and used by God that has turned away from Him.

Tumultuous Time Ahead
When these heads arise is a confusing issue. Esdra's prophecy says Biden's time is shorter than Trumps. How all this plays out is not known, but 2024 could certainly be a turbulent time. As described in the Foreward, we do not know with certainty if the Second Fulfillment of Daniel's Seventy Weeks began in 2020 or if it will begin in 2024.

The prophecy in Esdra appears to indicate that 2024 will be the time for the Antichrist to arrive, but we don't definitely know if our interpretation is correct. Regardless of the actual timing, everyone needs to be getting their spiritual house in order. Now is the time to make sure we are ready for what lies ahead. The next chapter will address this most important issue.

Chapter 3

THE TIMING OF THE RAPTURE

The Two Phases Jesus Taught

The timing of the rapture is one of the most controversial issues in the Church today. The traditional Pretribulation Rapture is the most popular view, but popularity should not be the measure of Scriptural truth. This author held the Pretribulation view until Marvin Rosenthal introduced his Pre-Wrath Rapture position. We believe his view may be partially correct; however, we also think that he is incorrect in thinking that God will not remove any believers before the start of the *great tribulation*.

Phased Rapture Position
We have come to believe that the Bible teaches that the Rapture will take place in two distinct phases where the Lord will remove His Firstfruit believers at the beginning followed by the removal of the remaining believers in the Main Harvest before God pours out His wrath. It is important to point out that Jesus taught the doctrine of a "phased" Rapture of believers in both the earlier and later parts of His ministry. First, in the Sermon on the Mount, Jesus taught His disciples to pray for deliverance from the Tribulation period (Matthew 6:13). At the very end of His ministry when He gives His famous discourse on the Mount of Olives, He also instructs His followers to always pray for escape from the same Tribulation period (Luke 21:34-36).

*34) And take heed to yourselves, lest at any time your hearts be overcharged with surfeiting, and drunkenness, and cares of this life, and so that day come upon you unawares. 35) For as a snare shall it come on all them that dwell on the face of the whole earth. 36) **Watch ye therefore, and <u>pray always</u>, that ye may be <u>accounted worthy</u> to <u>escape</u> all these things that shall come to pass, and to stand before the Son of man*** (Luke 21:34-36 – KJV).

Jesus chose to teach His disciples this principle of a "phased" Rapture because there is a way to escape the *great tribulation.* The first time on the Mount of Beatitudes when He gave the famous "Lord's prayer," He tells us: *"And do not lead us into temptation[3986] but deliver us from the evil one* (Matthew 6:13 – NIV). The Greek word for temptation is #3986 (peirasmos) which is the precise same term that Jesus uses in His promise to the Church of Philadelphia:

> Since you have kept my command ("word" – KJ) to endure patiently, *I will also keep you from the hour of trial[3986]* that is going to come upon the whole world to test those who live on the earth (Revelation 3:10 – NIV).

In other words, in the Lord's prayer, Jesus is telling us that we should be praying for God to deliver us from the coming trial of the Antichrist (evil one). This is the promise given to the Church of Philadelphia and it is also the same prayer mentioned above in His instructions on the Mount of Olives (*pray always to be accounted worthy to escape*).

Please notice that both times were on a *"Mount,"* both times He taught this *privately* to His disciples, and both times He included important instructions in a *prayer* for His disciples to follow. Jesus would not have taught us to pray to escape the coming Tribulation if it were not possible to do so. So while escape is possible, please notice that it is also very conditional. We need to *be accounted worthy to escape* (Luke 21:36) and we need to be *found keeping His word* (Revelation 3:10) to escape the coming tribulation period.

The faithful Philadelphian believer has the ears to hear and the heart to understand this teaching while most of the Church prefers to follow the Traditions of man (Colossians 2:8). The faithful, overcomer heeds the Lord's advice and continually *prays for deliverance* from the coming Tribulation period.

This teaching is not a new idea but was taught by many great men of God in the Philadelphia church age. Men like J. Hudson Taylor, Dr. A.B. Simpson, John Wilkison, Joseph A. Seiss, and Ray Brubaker. To learn more about this teaching please see *The Open Door* by Lyn Mize or download any of our free books at: www.ProphecyCountdown.com.

Now that we see that there is a way to escape the coming tribulation period, we need to see how this fits in with the fact that the tribulation will not be for the traditional period of 7 years as we have been taught.

We believe that the *great tribulation* is only 3 ½ years long and the traditional Pre-Trib, Mid-Trib, and Post-Trib Rapture positions can now be modified using the Phased Rapture approach with the faithful Firstfruit believers (accounted worthy) taken at the beginning followed by the rapture of the Main Harvest believers (lukewarm) at the end.

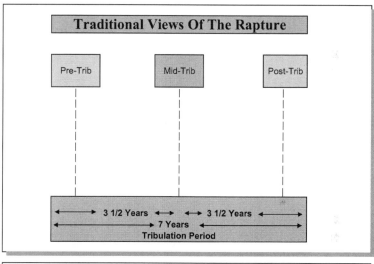

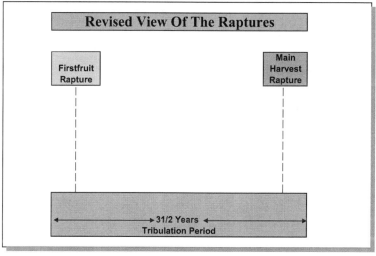

We need to remember that if Sultan Suleiman's decree in 1537, began the Second fulfillment of Daniel's Seventy-week prophecy then the final 70th Week began in 2020. This means that the Antichrist is due to appear very soon. Depending upon when in 2020 the final 7 years began, the mid-point could be anywhere between 2023 and 2024. The purpose of this booklet is not to set an exact date, but to alert the reader to the fact that time is very short and everyone needs to be preparing their hearts to meet Jesus today, while there is still time.

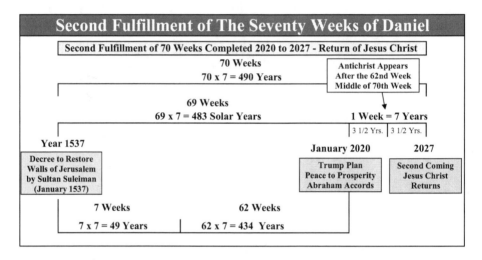

Parable of the Ten Virgins

The Great God of Heaven has announced in His Holy Word that a grand wedding is about to take place. Mankind's time on this earth is about up, and the Bridegroom is getting ready to return for His bride. Are you part of the bride of Christ? Will you be ready when Jesus returns? Who is it that is invited to the wedding banquet? It is those described in Revelation 19:7 and 9:

> *...For the wedding of the Lamb has come, and his bride has made herself ready...Then the angel said to me, "Write: Blessed are those who are invited to the wedding supper of the Lamb!" And he added "These are the true words of God* (Revelation 19:7,9 – NIV).

Notice that the above verse says, *"The bride made herself ready..."* How did she make herself ready?

> And to her it was granted to be arrayed in fine linen, clean
> and bright, for the *fine linen is the **righteous acts** of the saints*
> (Revelation 19:8 – NKJV).

The bride made herself ready for the wedding by obtaining her fine linen. This was her reward for the righteous life that she lived. The original Greek confirms that this fine linen is not the righteousness that is imputed to every believer in Christ but represents the righteous acts or the righteous living of the believer (conduct, acts, and deeds) following their salvation. This same teaching was confirmed for us by Jesus when He taught about the ten virgins:

> 1) Then the kingdom of heaven shall be likened to ten virgins who took their lamps and went out to meet the bridegroom. 2) Now five of them were wise, and five of them were foolish. Those who were foolish took their lamps and took no oil with them, 4) but the wise took oil in their vessels with their lamps. 5) But while the bridegroom was delayed, they all slumbered and slept. 6) And at midnight a cry was heard: 'Behold, the bridegroom is coming; go out to meet him!' 7) Then all those virgins arose and trimmed their lamps. 8) And the foolish said to the wise, 'Give us some of your oil, for our lamps, are going out.' 9) But the wise answered, saying, 'No, lest there should not be enough for us and you; but go rather to those who sell, and buy for yourselves.' 10) And while they went to buy, the bridegroom came, and those who were ready went in with him to the wedding; and the door was shut (Matthew 25:1-10 – NKJV).

Here we see that only the five wise virgins who were ready went to be with their Bridegroom. All 10 virgins were Christians because all did possess their oil, which represents the Holy Spirit who was given to each of them upon their conversion. The 5 foolish virgins, however, did not carry along the extra measure of oil that the 5 wise virgins carried in their jars. The 5 wise virgins were ready because they were obedient to the Word of God, which commands us to be *"filled with the Spirit"* (Ephesians 5:18). Because the 5 wise virgins were filled with the Spirit, they allowed Him to direct and empower their life.

It is important to note that the extra oil had to be bought by the foolish virgins (v.9). While the indwelling spirit is a free gift from God that cannot be bought, being filled by the Holy Spirit involves effort on the part of the Christian, requiring our submission to Him (Galatians 5:16-25) in order to crucify the flesh and allow Him complete control. As a result, the 5 wise virgins were properly equipped when the Bridegroom arrived. The wise virgins were ready because of their faithfulness, while the foolish virgins were not prepared due to their own lethargy in providing their extra measure of oil to keep their lamps burning.

Are you a wise or foolish virgin today? If you are not sure, please consider making the following prayer right now:

> "Dear God in Heaven, I realize that I have not really been living my life for you. I humbly turn to you right now and ask you to forgive me. Dear Jesus, please rule and reign in my heart and life. Please help me to live for you for whatever time remains. I pray that I may be accounted worthy and that I may be able to stand before you when you return. In Jesus' name, I pray. Amen"

Our prayer is that many who read this book will pray this prayer and ask the Lord to help them be prepared for His return. We know for certain Jesus will return very soon and we need to be ready every single day as we eagerly await His coming for us.

THE WISE VIRGINS
"They That Were Ready Went in with Him to the Marriage
and the Door Was Shut."

The above picture is from **The Second Coming of Christ**, by Clarence Larkin, p.17, © 1918-1922. Used with permission of the Rev. Clarence Larkin Estate, P.O. Box 334 Glenside, PA 19038, USA, 215-576-5590, www.larkinestate.com

Epilogue

If my analysis of the book of 2 Esdras is correct then this booklet represents a final warning for all of us. If I have made errors in any of my assumptions then this analysis may be another false alarm.

When the *great tribulation* period begins, you do not want to be here! As outlined in the last chapter, the Lord will keep some of His followers from experiencing that horrific time. Many believers may be relying on popular Church traditions or what popular authors teach, but very few may be removed when the decisive time arrives.

We need to remember that the great Apostle Paul was even concerned for himself when he taught us: *24) Do you not know that in a race all run, but one receives the prize? Run in such a way that you may obtain it....27) But I discipline my body and bring it into subjection, lest, when I have preached to others, **I myself should become disqualified** (1 Corinthians 9:24 &27 – NKJV).*

If Paul was concerned for himself, shouldn't we all be examining our own lives right now? Jesus told us to pray that ***we may be accounted worthy to escape*** the time that is coming. We all should be praying this for ourselves and helping those we love and care about while there is still time.

In our last book: ***The Final Countdown,*** we showed that Enoch's life served as a type-picture of the Firstfruit believer and since his rapture took place on the Feast of Pentecost (Enoch's birthday) it is a highly likely time for the Firstfruit rapture.

While I was attending the NRB convention in May of last year the Lord brought to my attention when the Feast of Pentecost will occur in 2024. I discovered a new Biblical Calendar from Israel that was produced by Galilee Calendars, Ltd. I had originally read that Pentecost for 2024 falls on June 13, which is the Orthodox date.

When I turned to the month of May I became extremely excited. On the 19th it stated:

> Pentecost Day USA – Traditional celebration of the descent of the Holy Spirit and the birth of the Church.[1]

The reason for my excitement (at the time) was this meant that my daughter Jennifer would be able to celebrate her 42nd birthday on the Feast of Pentecost! For those who are familiar with the meaning of numbers in the Bible, the number 42 is the number associated with the Rapture!

Jennifer had just turned 41 on May 19th when she was rushed to the hospital and placed on a ventilator. I became elated to think that on her next birthday in 2024, she would turn 42 on the Feast of Pentecost!

While she has already gone on ahead to her Heavenly home, could it be that we who are looking for the Lord's soon return, who are earnestly praying for the Lord to count us worthy to escape – that it may be the day we will join her for a real celebration!

*36) Watch ye therefore, and pray always, that ye may be **accounted worthy to escape** all these things that shall come to pass, and to stand before the Son of man* (Luke 21:36).

While we can not be certain that the Feast of Pentecost is the correct time for the rapture, the wise and faithful believers will take Matthew Henry's advice: *"Therefore every day and every hour we must be ready, and not off our watch any day in the year, or any hour in the day."* (Matthew Henry, Volume 5, p. 372)

If we are still here after May 19th we can rest assured in the promise that our Lord gave us: *"Because you have kept My command to persevere, I also will keep you from the hour of trial which shall come upon the whole world..."* (Revelation 3:10 – NKJV).

---

1) ***Biblical Calendars From Israel***, www.GalileeCalendars.com
16 Month Calendar-September 2023-December 2024 – 5783-5785

Bibliography

Commentaries on the Book of Daniel

Barnes, Albert – *Notes on the Bible: Daniel*, Baker Books © 1853 [Dan 9C] *

Carroll, B. H. – *An Interpretation of the English Bible: Daniel and the Inter-Biblical Period* (Available on Amazon or from: www.SolidChristianBooks.com) [Dan 9 C]**

Duguid, Ian M. – *Daniel*, P&R Publishers © 2008 [Dan 9C]

Emerson, Wallace L. – *Unlocking the Mysteries of Daniel*, Promise Publishing Co. © 1988 ***

Fausset, A.R. – *The Book of Daniel* (Available from the Blue Letter Bible (www.BlueLetterBible.org) [Dan 9C] *

Ferguson, Sinclair B. – *Daniel: The Preacher's Commentary*, Thomas Nelson Publishers © 1988 [Dan 9C] *

Hahn, Scott and Mitch, Curtis – *Daniel: The Ignatius Catholic Study Bible*, Ignatius Press © 1966 [Dan 9C] *

Henry, Matthew – *An Exposition: The Book of the Prophet Daniel*, Fleming H. Revell Co, Published in 1710 [Dan 9C]

Hewitt, Clarence H. – *The Seer of Babylon: Studies In The Book Of Daniel*, Kessinger Legacy Reprints, Advent Christian Publication Society © 1948 [Dan 9C] **

Jerome, St. – *Jerome's Commentary on Daniel* (translated by Gleason Archer), Wipf & Stock Publishers ©1958 [Dan 9C]

Miller, Stephen R. – *Daniel: The New American Commentary*, B&H Publishing Group © 1994 **

Mize, Lyn – *Daniel* (See link to **First Fruit Ministry** on the Bride tab at www.ProphecyCountdown.com) **

Thomson, J.E.H. – *The Pulpit Commentary: Daniel*, W.M. Eerdmans Publishing Co. © 1981 [Dan 9C] **

Walvoord, John F. – *Daniel*, Moody Publishers © 2012

Young, Edward J. – *The Prophecy of Daniel*, W.M. Eerdmans Publishing Co. © 1949 [Dan 9C] **

[Dan 9C] Daniel 9 is rightly shown as Christ, not the Antichrist.

 * Most useful commentaries in this author's opinion.

Other Books Quoted or Consulted

Bercot, David W. – *A Dictionary of Early Christian Beliefs*, Hendricks Publishers © 2019

Coerper, Steve – *The "Daily [Sacrifice]" or "The Blameless"?*, Anakypto Forum Article, www.RogerShermanSociety.org

Deal, Colin – *The Great Tribulation: How Long?*, End Time News © 1991, P.O. Box 455, Rutherford College, NC 28671 [Dan 9C]

Galilee Calendars, Ltd. – *Biblical Calendars of the Old Testament*, www.GalileeCalendars.com © 2023,1-866-743-3320 USA toll-free

Jones, Dr. Floyd Nolen – *The Chronology of the Old Testament*, Master Books © 1993, New Leaf Press © 2005 [Also see the *Supplemental Articles* for *Daniel's Prophecies Unsealed.*]

Larkin, Rev. Clarence – *Second Coming of Christ*, Rev. Clarence Larkin Estate © 1918-1922. The picture shown in this book is used with permission of the Rev. Clarence Larkin Estate: P.O. Box 334, Glenside, PA 19038, USA, www.larkinestate.com

Mize, Lyn – *The Open Door*, Prophecy Countdown Publications, LLC © 2022, www.ProphecyCountdown.com

Myers, Jacob M. – *The Anchor Bible: I and II Esdras, Introduction, Translation and Commentary*, Doubleday & Company © 1974

New Oxford Annotated Apocrypha, Oxford University Press © 1991

Panton, D. M. – *The Judgment Seat of Christ*, Schoettle Publishing Co. Inc., © 1984, www.schoettlepublishing.com

Schobl-Legee, Rev. Barbara – *Prophecy About Biden: Bye, Bye, Biden!*, Legee Publishing © 2023

Schwab, Timothy – *The Book of 2 Esdras The Hidden Book of Prophecy*, The Levite Bible © 2021

Shupe, Pastor Randy – *Babylon the Great*, Apostolic Missions, Inc. © 2007 (www.PastorRandyShupe.com)

Widener, Christian – *Witnessing The End: Daniel's Seventy Sevens and the Final Decree Everyone Missed*, End Times Berean © 2022, www.WitnessingtheEnd.com

Widener, Christian – *The Temple Revealed*, End Times Berean © 2022, www.EndTimesBerean.com

[Dan 9C] Daniel 9 is rightly shown as Christ, not the Antichrist.

Appendix 1 – Summary of the Eight Little Wings

Once *The Final Countdown* was completed we discovered additional confirmations that the main thesis of this book may indeed be correct. One such validation occurred while attending the NRB convention in May 2023. In a breakaway session on the Abraham Accords, two former Ambassadors from Morocco and UAE who were involved in the peace agreements of 2020 confirmed very strongly that it was God and Trump who "did it!" The Second fulfillment of Daniel's Seventy Weeks clearly began in the year 2020.

The second corroboration was just recently found in a book of the Apocrypha entitled: 2 Esdras. This little-known book was part of the original Authorized King James Bible (A.V.) in 1611. In 1885 the Revised Version (R.V.) replaced the Authorized Version, and the Apocrypha was removed. Remarkably, the 11th and 12th chapters of this ancient book contain an amazing prophetic vision of "The Eagle," which we know from our studies in chapter 7 of the book of Daniel is the United States of America!

This mysterious little book may hold an important clue regarding the events being witnessed during these closing days. The chart found on page ix shows the Second Fulfillment of the Seventy Weeks of Daniel, which illustrates how the final 7-years began with the peace accords in 2020 and end with the Second Coming of Christ in 2027. This would mean that the Antichrist should appear sometime between now and the middle of 2024. If this is correct it would mean that this year's elections will be interrupted. This would mean that Joe Biden will be replaced by the Antichrist and that his term in office will not complete the normal four-year period.

As you will find in the following analysis of Esdras vision, Trump's term is followed by Biden's, which will be cut short. This is because Esdras's vision is telling us that the 3 heads of the Eagle will appear before Biden's second term. These 3 heads of the Eagle will rule the earth during these final closing days of *great tribulation*.

Prophecy in 2 Esdras 11 and 12
God Raises the Antichrist

22) And after this, I looked and saw the twelve wings and the two little wings had disappeared 23) and nothing remained on the eagle's body except the *three heads*[1] that were at rest and the **six** little wings.

24) As I kept looking I saw that **two** little wings[a&5] **separated** from the **six** and remained under the head that was on the right side; but **four** remained in their place.

25) Then I saw that these little wings (H. Clinton and T. Kane)[b] *planned* to set themselves up and hold the rule.
26) As I kept looking, one was set up (Trump), but suddenly disappeared; 27) a second also, (Biden) and this disappeared more quickly than the first [less than 4-year term].

28) While I continued to look the **two** that remained (President Candidate and VP Candidate)[c] were *planning* between themselves to **reign together**; 29) and while they were *planning*, one of the **heads** that were at rest (the one that was in the middle)[2] suddenly **awoke**; [Does God raise the Antichrist from the grave?] it was greater than the other *two heads* [see footnote #3]

30) And I saw how it **allied** the *two heads*[3] with itself, 31) and how the head turned with those that were with it and devoured the two little wings (President and VP Candidates)[c] that were *planning* to reign.

32) Moreover <u>this head gained control of the whole earth</u>, and with much oppression dominated its inhabitants; it had greater power over the world than all the wings that had gone before.

33) After this I looked again and saw the head in the middle suddenly disappear, just as the wings had done. 34) But the two heads remained[4] (Antichrist and False Prophet), which in like manner ruled over the earth and its inhabitants. (2 Esdras 11:22-34)

Note: The **speculations** *in this analysis are not meant to assert dogmatic identities of the various leaders involved.* **We do not know** *for sure who God will use to orchestrate His final plan, but we believe this little-known book could provide us with some important clues.*

NRSV – New Oxford Apocrypha, Oxford University Press © 1991

Footnotes to Appendix 1

a 2 Esdras 11:24 is interpreted in 2 Esdras 12:29: *"It is these (two little wings) whom the Most High has kept for the eagle's end."* This is the time of the **great tribulation**.

b Verse 23 ends with three heads and six little wings. Verse 24 shows that two of these wings who did not rule separated from the six (see footnote #5). Verse 25 then introduces **two** wings who were *planning* to set themselves up to run for president and vice president after Obama's term ended. We know these two people were Hillary Clinton and Tim Kane who ran for office in 2016 (planned to hold the rule) but did not rule.

c Someone has suggested that the two that remained in verse 28, should be the President and VP Candidates. They would be the ones who are *planning* between themselves to **reign together**. If anyone has any other ideas of who these two candidates could possibly be, please send your ideas to the author at JimHarmanCPA@gmail and we will consider revising this.

1) 2 Esdras 12:22-25: *"22) As for your seeing **three heads** at rest, this is the interpretation: 23) In its last days the Most High will **raise up three kings**, and they shall renew many things in it, and **shall rule the earth** 24) and its inhabitants more oppressively than all who were before them. Therefore they are called the **heads of the eagle** because it is they who shall sum up his wickedness and **perform his last actions**.*

2) The **head in the middle** was greater than the others and stands for the **Antichrist**, whom God raises up for the final 3 ½ years.

3) Verses 33-34, describe the other **two heads**: **Prince Charles**** is the leader of the Lion (England), which is the 1st beast in Daniel 7:4, he could become one of the **three heads** of the eagle in Esdras 11:23. The 4th beast in Daniel 7:7, which will be led by the **Antichrist** (little horn), will also be **allied** with the **False Prophet**, who is another of the three heads.
   ** Some believe one of the 3 heads could be **Barack Obama**.

4) The two heads that remained in 2 Esdras 11:34 are explained in 2 Esdras 12:26-27: *"26) As for your seeing that the large head disappeared, one of the kings shall die in his bed* (**Prince Charles or Obama**), *but in agonies. 27) But as for the two who remained* (**Antichrist** and the **False Prophet**), *the sword shall devour them."* (This will take place at the very end of the **great tribulation** period as described in Revelation 19:20-21).

5) 2 Esdras 12:19-21: *"19) As for your seeing **eight little wings** clinging to its wings, this is the interpretation: 20) **Eight <u>kings</u>** shall arise in it, whose <u>time shall be short and their years swift</u>; 21) **two** of them shall perish when the middle of its time draws near;* (President and VP Candidates to perish in the very middle of the Seven year period between 2020 and 2027) *and **four** shall be kept for the time when its end approaches* (Hillary Clinton, Tim Kane, Donald Trump, and Joe Biden), *but **<u>two shall be kept until the end</u>*** (Obama? and Clinton?)."

[2 Esdras 12:29: *"It is these (two little wings) whom the Most High has kept for the eagle's end."*]

The **eight little wings** that are described here represent the eight *"rival wings,"* mentioned in 2 Esdras 11:11. This helps explain how there are two wings that **separated** from the six, making a total of **eight wings** (interpreted as **kings**):

6) 2 Esdras 12:31-33 describes how **Jesus** is the Lion roused from the forest. He will come to judge and destroy these **three heads of the Eagle.**

Chronological Order of Wings

This brief analysis of 2 Esdras 11 and 12, began after the first 14 wings had completed their reign as shown in 2 Esdras 11:22:

> *22) And after this, I looked and saw the **twelve** wings and the **two** little wings had disappeared.*

The **first** 14 wings started with Herbert Hoover in 2 Esdras 11:12-13. We know this because the **second** wing is easily detected as Franklin Delano Roosevelt (FDR) who was in office for over 12 years and he is described as follows: *"The next wing rose up and reigned, and it continued to reign a **long time**…I announce to you before you disappear. After you **no one shall rule as long as you** have ruled…"* (2 Esdras 11:13,16,17) Ever since then the President can only hold office for a maximum of 8 years. Since Herbert Hoover (31st President) was the **first wing** mentioned, the **14th wing** would be Barack Obama (44th President).

Appendix 2 – Esdras 11 & 12
New Revised Standard

2 Esdras 11

The fifth vision; description of the vision

1 On the second night I had a dream: I saw rising from the sea an eagle that had twelve feathered wings and three heads. 2 I saw it spread its wings over the whole earth, and all the winds of heaven blew upon it, and the clouds were gathered around it. 3 I saw that out of its wings there grew opposing wings; but they became little, puny wings. 4 But its heads were at rest; the middle head was larger than the other heads, but it too was at rest with them. 5 Then I saw that the eagle flew with its wings, and it reigned over the earth and over those who inhabit it. 6 And I saw how all things under heaven were subjected to it, and no one spoke against it — not a single creature that was on the earth. 7 Then I saw the eagle rise upon its talons, and it uttered a cry to its wings, saying, 8 "Do not all watch at the same time; let each sleep in its own place, and watch in its turn; 9 but let the heads be reserved for the last."

10 I looked again and saw that the voice did not come from its heads, but from the middle of its body. 11 I counted its rival wings, and there were eight of them. 12 As I watched, one wing on the right side rose up, and it reigned over all the earth. 13 And after a time its reign came to an end, and it disappeared, so that even its place was no longer visible. Then the next wing rose up and reigned, and it continued to reign a long time. 14 While it was reigning its end came also, so that it disappeared like the first. 15 And a voice sounded, saying to it, 16 "Listen to me, you who have ruled the earth all this time; I announce this to you before you disappear. 17 After you no one shall rule as long as you have ruled, not even half as long."

18 Then the third wing raised itself up, and held the rule as the earlier ones had done, and it also disappeared. 19 And so it went with all the wings; they wielded power one after another and then were never seen

again. 20 I kept looking, and in due time the wings that followed also rose up on the right side, in order to rule. There were some of them that ruled, yet disappeared suddenly; 21 and others of them rose up, but did not hold the rule.

22 And after this I looked and saw that the twelve wings and the two little wings had disappeared, 23 and nothing remained on the eagle's body except the three heads that were at rest and six little wings.

24 As I kept looking I saw that two little wings separated from the six and remained under the head that was on the right side; but four remained in their place. 25 Then I saw that these little wings planned to set themselves up and hold the rule. 26 As I kept looking, one was set up, but suddenly disappeared; 27 a second also, and this disappeared more quickly than the first. 28 While I continued to look the two that remained were planning between themselves to reign together; 29 and while they were planning, one of the heads that were at rest (the one that was in the middle) suddenly awoke; it was greater than the other two heads. 30 And I saw how it allied the two heads with itself, 31 and how the head turned with those that were with it and devoured the two little wings that were planning to reign. 32 Moreover this head gained control of the whole earth, and with much oppression dominated its inhabitants; it had greater power over the world than all the wings that had gone before.

33 After this I looked again and saw the head in the middle suddenly disappear, just as the wings had done. 34 But the two heads remained, which also in like manner ruled over the earth and its inhabitants. 35) And while I looked, I saw the head on the right side devour the one on the left. 36 Then I heard a voice saying to me, "Look in front of you and consider what you see." 37 When I looked, I saw what seemed to be a lion roused from the forest, roaring; and I heard how it uttered a human voice to the eagle, and spoke, saying, 38 "Listen and I will speak to you.

The Most High says to you, 39 'Are you not the one that remains of the four beasts that I had made to reign in my world, so that the end of my times might come through them? 40 You, the fourth that has come, have conquered all the beasts that have gone before; and you have held sway over the world with great terror, and over all the earth with grievous oppression; and for so long you have lived on the earth with deceit. 41 You have judged the earth, but not with truth, 42 for you have oppressed the meek and injured the peaceable; you have hated those who tell the truth, and have loved liars; you have destroyed the homes of those who brought forth fruit, and have laid low the walls of those who did you no harm. 43 Your insolence has come up before the Most High, and your pride to the Mighty One. 44 The Most High has looked at his times; now they have ended, and his ages have reached completion. 45 Therefore you, eagle, will surely disappear, you and your terrifying wings, your most evil little wings, your malicious heads, your most evil talons, and your whole worthless body, 46 so that the whole earth, freed from your violence, may be refreshed and relieved, and may hope for the judgment and mercy of him who made it.'"

2 Esdras 12

1 While the lion was saying these words to the eagle, I looked 2 and saw that the remaining head had disappeared. The two wings that had gone over to it rose up and set themselves up to reign, and their reign was brief and full of tumult. 3 When I looked again, they were already vanishing. The whole body of the eagle was burned, and the earth was exceedingly terrified.

The seer's response
Then I woke up in great perplexity of mind and great fear, and I said to my spirit, 4 "You have brought this upon me, because you search out the ways of the Most High. 5 I am still weary in mind and very weak in my spirit, and not even a little strength is left in me, because of the great fear with which I have been terrified tonight. 6 Therefore I will now entreat the Most High that he may strengthen me to the end."

7 Then I said, "O sovereign Lord, if I have found favor in your sight, and if I have been accounted righteous before you beyond many others, and if my prayer has indeed come up before your face, 8 strengthen me and show me, your servant, the interpretation and meaning of this terrifying vision so that you may fully comfort my soul. 9 For you have judged me worthy to be shown the end of the times and the last events of the times."

The interpretation
10 He said to me, "This is the interpretation of this vision that you have seen: 11 The eagle that you saw coming up from the sea is the fourth kingdom that appeared in a vision to your brother Daniel. 12 But it was not explained to him as I now explain to you or have explained it. 13 The days are coming when a kingdom shall rise on earth, and it shall be more terrifying than all the kingdoms that have been before it. 14 And twelve kings shall reign in it, one after another. 15 But the second that is to reign shall hold sway for a longer time than any other one of the twelve. 16 This is the interpretation of the twelve wings that you saw.

17 "As for your hearing a voice that spoke, coming not from the eagle's heads but from the midst of its body, this is the interpretation: 18 In the midst of the time of that kingdom great struggles shall arise, and it shall be in danger of falling; nevertheless it shall not fall then, but shall regain its former power. 19 As for your seeing eight little wings clinging to its wings, this is the interpretation: 20 Eight kings shall arise in it, whose times shall be short and their years swift; 21 two of them shall perish when the middle of its time draws near; and four shall be kept for the time when its end approaches, but two shall be kept until the end.

22 "As for your seeing three heads at rest, this is the interpretation:

23 In its last days the Most High will raise up three kings, and they shall renew many things in it, and shall rule the earth 24 and its inhabitants more oppressively than all who were before them. Therefore they are called the heads of the eagle, 25 because it is they who shall sum up his wickedness and perform his last actions.

26 As for your seeing that the large head disappeared, one of the kings shall die in his bed, but in agonies. 27 But as for the two who remained, the sword shall devour them. 28 For the sword of one shall devour him who was with him; but he also shall fall by the sword in the last days.

29 "As for your seeing two little wings passing over to the head which was on the right side, 30 this is the interpretation: It is these whom the Most High has kept for the eagle's end; this was the reign which was brief and full of tumult, as you have seen.

31 "And as for the lion whom you saw rousing up out of the forest and roaring and speaking to the eagle and reproving him for his unrighteousness, and as for all his words that you have heard, 32 this is the Messiah whom the Most High has kept until the end of days, who will arise from the offspring of David, and will come and speak with them. He will denounce them for their ungodliness and for their wickedness, and will display before them their contemptuous dealings.33 For first he will bring them alive before his judgment seat, and when he has reproved them, then he will destroy them. 34 But in mercy he will set free the remnant of my people, those who have been saved throughout my borders, and he will make them joyful until the end comes, the day of judgment, of which I spoke to you at the beginning. 35 This is the dream that you saw, and this is its interpretation. 36 And you alone were worthy to learn this secret of the Most High.

Conclusion and injunctions
37 Therefore write all these things that you have seen in a book, put it in a hidden place; 38 and you shall teach them to the wise among your people, whose hearts you know are able to comprehend and keep these secrets. 39 But as for you, wait here seven days more, so that you may be shown whatever it pleases the Most High to show you."

Then he left me.

The seer comforts those who were grieved because of his absence
40 When all the people heard that the seven days were past and I had not returned to the city, they all gathered together, from the least to the greatest, and came to me and spoke to me, saying, 41 "How have we offended you, and what harm have we done you, that you have forsaken us and sit in this place? 42 For of all the prophets you alone are left to us, like a cluster of grapes from the vintage, and like a lamp in a dark place, and like a haven for a ship saved from a storm. 43 Are not the disasters that have befallen us enough? 44 Therefore if you forsake us, how much better it would have been for us if we also had been consumed in the burning of Zion. 45 For we are no better than those who died there." And they wept with a loud voice.

Then I answered them and said, 46 "Take courage, O Israel; and do not be sorrowful, O house of Jacob; 47 for the Most High has you in remembrance, and the Mighty One has not forgotten you in your struggle. 48 As for me, I have neither forsaken you nor withdrawn from you; but I have come to this place to pray on account of the desolation of Zion, and to seek mercy on account of the humiliation of our sanctuary. 49 Now go to your homes, every one of you, and after these days I will come to you." 50 So the people went into the city, as I told them to do. 51 But I sat in the field seven days, as the angel had commanded me; and I ate only of the flowers of the field, and my food was of plants during those days.

Appendix 3 – Esdras 11 & 12
The Anchor Bible

2 Esdras 11

1 Then, in the second night, I had a dream [in which] I saw an eagle coming up out of the sea; it had twelve feathered wings and three heads. 2 As I kept looking, it spread out its wings over the whole earth, so all the winds of heaven blew upon it and the clouds gathered around it. 3 Moreover, I observed rival wings spring up out of its wings that became puny and petty wings. 4 But its heads were dormant, the middle head was larger than the other heads though it too was dormant as they were. 5 Then I saw that the eagle flew with its wings to gain dominion over the earth and its inhabitants. 6 I saw, too, how everything under heaven was subjected to it so that no one resisted it – not a single creature on earth. 7 As I kept looking, the eagle rose upon its talons and spoke to its wings as follows; 8 Do not all stand guard at the same time, sleep each one in its place and stand guard in turn; 9 but *the heads are to be kept till last.* 10 When I looked again, I noticed that the voice did not come from its heads but from the middle of its body. 11 I counted its rival wings and found there were eight [of them]. 12 When I looked on the right side I saw one wing rise and it held sway over the whole earth. 13 Then after its rule ended it disappeared so that even its place was no longer visible. Then the next one rose up and held sway for a long time. As its rule came to its end and it disappeared, just like [its] predecessor, 15 a voice spoke to it as follows: 16 Listen you, you who have held sway over the earth for such [a long] time, to this proclamation before you are about to depart 17 No one after you will hold sway for so long as you [did]. not even half as long. 18 Then the third [wing] elevated itself, held sway like [its] predecessors but it too disappeared.
19 And so it was with all the wings, each one in turn assuming leadership and then likewise disappearing.

20 As I kept looking I saw in the course of time, the other wings on the right side set themselves up to take leadership; some of them held sway but disappeared at once,   21 while others of them set themselves

up but did not achieve leadership. 22 Later I looked and saw that the twelve wings and the two winglets had disappeared, 23 so that nothing was left of the eagle's body except the three dormant heads and the six little wings. 24 As I kept looking I saw that two of the six winglets disengaged themselves [from the rest], and remained under the head that was on the right side while the four remained in their place.

25 Then I observed that these sub-wings plotted to set themselves up to achieve leadership, 26 As I kept on looking, one set itself up but disappeared at once; 27 then a second, and it disappeared more rapidly than the preceding one. 28 While I continued to look the two remaining ones themselves plotted to assume rule. 29 At the time they were plotting, one of the dormant heads – the one in the middle and larger than the other two – awoke.

30 Then I observed how the two [other] heads were conjoined with it 31 and [how] the head with its conjoiners turned and devoured the two sub-wings that plotted to rule. 32 This head subdued the whole earth, held ruthless sway over all its inhabitants and exercised more power over the world than all the wings that preceded it.

33 After this I looked again and saw the head in the middle disappear suddenly, just as the wings had done. 34 However, the two heads that held sway over the earth and those who inhabited it remained.

35 While I was looking I saw the head on the right side devour the one on the left. 36 Then I heard a voice saying to me: Look in front of you and contemplate what you see. 37 When I looked I saw what appeared like a raging lion [coming] roaring out of the forest and I heard it talk in human language to the eagle. It spoke as follows:

38 Now you listen and I will speak to you The Most High declares to you: 39 Are you not the *only one of the four beasts left* that I appointed to hold sway over my world so that through them the end of my times might come? 40 You are the fourth that has come and you have subdued, all the preceding beasts,

Holding sway over the world with great terror,
And over the entire earth with the utmost oppression;
You lived for so long in the world with duplicity;

41 You have not judged the earth with truth.
42 You have oppressed the meek,
You have injured the peaceful,
You have hated those who speak the truth,
You have loved liars,
You have destroyed the homes of the thrifty,
You have razed the walls of those who did you no harm.
43 Your arrogance has reached the Most High,
And your haughtiness the Almighty.
44 The Most High has considered his times;
Now they have come to an end;
His ages have attained completion.
45 Therefore, *you eagle, you will vanish,*
With your horrible wings,
With your evil winglets,
With your malicious heads,
With your ghastly talons,
With your whole sinister body.
46 Thus the whole earth will be relieved and delivered from our power; then it can hope for justice and the compassion of him who made it.

2 Esdras 12

1 While the lion was speaking these words to the eagle, I looked 2 and saw that the remaining head had vanished. Then the two wings which had gone over to it arose and set themselves up to rule but their reign was weak and tumultuous. When I looked again they had vanished, the entire body of the eagle went up in flames and the earth was aghast.

Request for an interpretation of the vision
a.   Weakened by his dream-vision ordeal, Ezra pleads for strength

Then I awoke because of intense excitement and great fear, and said to myself; See here, you are responsible for this experience of mine because you are prying into the ways of the Most High.

    5 Besides, I am mentally exhausted,
    And I am greatly impoverished in spirit;

there is not left in me the slightest strength by virtue of the great fear I encountered this night. Now, therefore, I will pray to the Most High to uphold me to the end.

b. Ezra's prayer

7 So I said, O Lord, Lord, if you please, if I am accounted by you more just than the many, and if my prayer has assuredly come up before you, 8 uphold me and disclose to me, your servant, the interpretation and meaning of this awful vision so as to put my mind completely at ease. 9 You have already regarded me worthy to be shown the end of days and the conclusion of times.

c. Interpretation of the vision

10 Then he answered me: This is the interpretation of this vision that you saw. 11 The eagle you observed coming up out of the sea is the fourth kingdom that appeared in a vision to Daniel, your brother.
12. But it was not interpreted to him in the same way that I now interpret [it]. 13 Indeed, days are coming when a kingdom will rise on earth that will be more dreadful than all the kingdoms that existed before it. 14 Twelve kings will hold sway over it, one after another. 15 the second to assume power will hold [it] longer than [any other one of] the twelve. 16 This is the interpretation of the twelve wings you saw. 17 About the voice you heard speaking, which did not come from its heads but from the middle of its body, 18 this is the interpretation: Following the period of that king's reign no inconsiderable struggles will arise so that it will be threatened with falling, yet it will not fall then but again recover its earlier [power]. 19 About the eight sub-wings you saw springing from its wings, 20 this is the interpretation: eight kings will arise in it whose times will be short and whose years will pass quickly, *two of them falling* 21 *close to the middle of its time*, while four will be reserved for the time when it end-time draws near; two, however, will be preserved for the end.

22 About the three dormant heads you saw, 23 this is the interpretation; in its final days the Most High will raise up three kings who will restore many things in it and exercise dominion over the earth 24 and its inhabitants with greater harshness than all who were before

them. For this reason they have been called eagle's heads, 25 because they are the ones who will bring his [the eagle's] ungodliness to a head and bring about his end. 26 About the larger head you saw disappearing – one of them will die on his bed but nevertheless in anguish. 27 As for the two remaining ones, the sword will consume them. 28 For the sword of the one will consume his companion but in the end he too will fall by the sword. 29 About the two sub-wings you saw going over to the head on the right side, 30 this is the interpretation: these are the ones the Most High has reserved for its end; this rule will be short and full of turbulence, 31 as you saw. The raging lion which you saw [coming] roaring out of the forest, speaking to the eagle, taking it to task for its injustice, and all its words which you heard, 32 he is the anointed one who the Most High has reserved till the end of days, who will arise from the seed of David, come and speak with them,

> Upbraid them for their wickedness,
>
> Condemn them for their injustices,
>
> And confront them directly with their insults.

33 First he will present them alive for judgment, and then, after up-braiding them, he will destroy them. 34 But the remnant for my people who are left in my land he will set free with compassion and grant them joy until the end, the day of judgment about which I spoke to you at the beginning. 35 This is the dream you saw and this is the interpretation.

Esdra's Three-Headed Eagle
Illustration of the three-headed Eagle
From Ezra's Vision of Daniel's Fourth Beast

Appendix 4 – Daniel's Fourth Beast

The identity of the fourth beast in Daniel's vision described in Daniel 7 is found in the book of Revelation, as well as another unfamiliar prophecy written in the Apocrypha.

Apocrypha

First, we will look at the book of 2 Esdras, which is one of the books in the Apocrypha. This little-known book was part of the original Authorized King James Bible (A.V.) in 1611. In 1885 the Revised Version (R.V.) replaced the Authorized Version, and the Apocrypha was removed. While this book has not been given the same weight as Scripture, we discovered a remarkable reference describing Daniel's **4th beast** of Daniel 7.

> *...1) I had a dream I saw <u>rising from the sea</u> an <u>eagle</u>...2) I saw it spread its wings <u>over the whole earth</u>...5) and it <u>reigned over the earth</u> and over those who inhabit it...6) all things under heaven were subjected to it, and no one spoke against it–not a single creature...on the earth.* (2 Esdras 11:1, 2, 5, & 6)

> *10) He said to me, "This is the <u>interpretation of this vision</u> that you have seen: 11) the <u>eagle</u> that you saw coming up from the sea is the <u>fourth kingdom</u> that appeared in a <u>vision</u> to your brother <u>Daniel</u>.* (2 Esdras 12:10-11)

The above prophecy included in the Apocrypha declares the **fourth beast** of Daniel is represented to be an **eagle**! Of course, the **eagle** is the symbol of the United States of America.

John's Apocalypse

Daniel's **4th beast** is also explained in John's portrayal of Mystery Babylon in the book of Revelation, which is described in the following section.

Mystery Explained (Revelation 17:7-18)

The angel tells John the clues to solve the mystery surrounding the harlot seen riding on the beast with 7 heads and 10 horns (Rev 17:7). On the facing page is a summary of the key verses, along with this author's speculation of the identity of the nations involved.

Verse 8 – At the time John wrote this, the beast that "was" and "is not" must be Babylon, which fell in 539 BC. It could not be Rome since the Romans came into power in 63 BC with Pompey's occupation of Jerusalem.

Verse 9 – This verse, along with verse 18, reveals that the 7 heads are 7 hills or mountains upon which their headquarters are located.[1] Verse 9 states that understanding the true identity of this important city calls for wisdom. We know these cities will be the headquarters of the Beast and the harlot. Since the city of Rome is well known as *"the city on 7 hills,"* we know this is where the harlot is located.

Verse 10 – The 7 kings include the 5 who have fallen (Egypt, Assyria, Babylon, Persia, and Greece, + Rome (which was in power at the time John wrote this), leaving the Beast, who has not yet come (we deem is the New Babylon: Daniel's 4th Beast).

Verse 11 – The Beast that "was" and "is not" is of the 7 that are listed. From verses 8 and 10 above we see this must be from the Beast named New Babylon (the 7th). The actual Antichrist is the *"little horn"* which comes out of the 7th one listed (*cf.* Dan 7:7-8). This *"little horn"* is the 8th and will be destroyed at the very end (*cf.* Rev 19:20).

The Beast will rule from the center of economic and political power. New York City is probably the greatest commercial and banking center in the world. It is also the headquarters for the United Nations, which could host the global government to place all sovereign nations under the Beast's control, in order to bring in the New World Order (NWO). Interestingly, New York will become ***"the city on 7 mountains,"*** since the Beast will have dominion over ***"the seven continents"*** of the world. Both the Beast and the harlot (False Prophet) will rule the world from their strategic command centers: New York and Rome.

Mystery of Woman, Beast and 10 Horns

"7) But the angel said to me, 'Why did you marvel? **I will tell you the mystery** *of the* **woman*** *and of the* **beast** *that* **carries her**, *which has the* **seven heads and the ten horns**.

8) The beast that you saw **was**, *and is* **not**, *and* **will ascend** *out of the bottomless pit and go to perdition.* **And those who dwell on the earth will marvel**... *when they see the beast that was, and is not, and yet is.*

Beast Was	Beast Is Not	Beast Will Ascend
Babylon	Babylon	*(Daniel's 4th Beast)*

9) 'Here is the mind which has wisdom: The seven heads are seven mountains on which the woman sits.

10) There are also seven kings. Five have fallen, one is, and the other has not yet come. And when he comes, he must continue a short time.

5 Kings Have Fallen	One Is	Not Yet Come
Egypt, Assyria Babylon, Persia Greece	Rome	Beast *(4th Beast)*

11) 'The beast that was, and is not, is himself also the eighth, and is of the seven, and is going to perdition.

5 5 Kings Have Fallen	**6** One Is	**7** Not Yet Come	**8** He is of The 7
Egypt, Assyria Babylon, Persia Greece	Rome	Beast *(4th Beast)* [7 Heads & 10 Horns]	Little Horn (comes out of the 7)

18) 'And the **woman*** *whom you saw is that* **great city which reigns over the kings of the earth.'"*

(Revelation 17:7-11, 18)

* Cities = New York City and Rome: the Headquarters for the U.N. / America and the Roman Catholic Church.

From the foregoing description of *Mystery Babylon*, we see that Daniel's 4th beast is the **seventh** kingdom that had not existed when the Apostle John penned these words. This means that Daniel's 4th beast must be an **entirely new** kingdom to arrive (**it's not**: Egypt, Assyria, Babylon, Persia, Greece, or Rome). We believe this embodies America which symbolizes a New Babylon. This new 4th beast is different from all of the other beasts because it is an amalgamation of America aligned with 10 other nations led by the Antichrist (Little Horn).

Readers desiring additional evidence for America being part of Mystery Babylon should read our commentary on the book of Revelation: *Calling All Overcomers*. This can be freely downloaded on our website: www.ProphecyCountdown.com

We also highly recommend Pastor Randy Shupe's excellent analysis of this subject in his volume: *Babylon the Great*. This exceptional book is available at: www.PastorRandyShupe.com

Finally, as was explained at the beginning of this appendix, we cannot ignore the remarkable description of our beloved nation of America (the Eagle) found in the Apocrypha. While this account has not been held with the same importance as Scripture, we should not ignore a prophecy that was included by King James when he authorized the Apocrypha to be included in the Holy Bible of 1611.

While the speculations in this booklet are not meant to dogmatically identify the various nations associated with the prophecies, we believe God included essential information in his Holy Word to alert believers during the time of the end.

*"And I heard another voice from heaven saying, '**Come out of her, my people,** lest you share in her sins, and lest you receive of her plagues'"* (Revelation 18:4).

Appendix 5

BABYLON THE GREAT
The Last Great Nation

My goal [in this book] is to seek to unlock the threefold imagery of the depiction of Mystery Babylon as "a woman sitting on a beast which has ten horns" (Rev 17). The premise I am setting before you is that this threefold imagery is America as the beast, Catholicism as the religious harlot woman riding the beast, and the EU as the ten horns of the beast. This scenario could be dismissed as mere speculation apart from the existence of a unifying common denominator linking all three together. Let us consider that common bond. America, Catholicism and the EU have a historical and cultural thread that links them together: all three are Roman in origin. Mystery Babylon is Roman to the core. Scriptures teach that the last great world empire that will be on the face of the earth just prior to the second coming of Jesus Christ is a kingdom that has its roots in the Roman Empire. It is this common denominator that links them together as one identity namely, Mystery Babylon.

Pastor Randy Shupe – *Babylon The Great*

Scripture records three Babylons. The first Babylon was Ancient Babylon ruled over by Nebuchadnezzar and conquered by the Medes and Persians in 539 B.C. Ancient Babylon was never destroyed like the Biblical description of the destruction of the New Babylon described in Revelation 18 and Jeremiah 50 and 51. Thus, Ancient Babylon and New Babylon are two distinct places with different geographical locations and distinctive characteristics.

The second Babylon recorded in Scripture is Ecclesiastical or Religious Babylon. This Babylon is the harlot church described in Revelation 17 and headed up by the False Prophet of Revelation 13. The identity of Religious Babylon has been known for hundreds of years and a sincere reading of the Scriptures reveals that the Papal Worship System is the Great Harlot of Revelation 17. It is no longer any secret among prophetic scholars that John Paul II is also the False Prophet of Revelation 13.

There are several books that thoroughly document the identity of the Great Whore of Babylon as the Papal Worship System incorporated into the Roman Catholic Church like the working of leaven in dough. Peter Lalonde's book, *One World Under Antichrist* is an excellent example. Also, Dave Hunt's book, *Global Peace* identifies John Paul II as the False Prophet, and Pastor Randy Shupe's volume *Babylon the Great* gives an excellent, in-depth analysis of the three components of this end-time mystery.

John Paul II came up out of Poland, and the name Poland literally means "the people of the earth". The miter the Pope wears has two points on it that strongly resemble horns. Thus, John Paul II came up out of the earth and he has two horns like a lamb (Rev 13:11). He also came to the papacy with full knowledge and appreciation of the geopolitical power of his position.

It was revealed in "Newsweek" magazine in late 1990 that President Bush and Soviet Premier Mikhail Gorbachev consulted with the Pope on a weekly basis. Soviet Foreign Minister Gromyko described the Pope as a man with a weltanschauung (i.e., world view). Also, President Clinton flew to Denver, Colorado expressly to visit with the Pope. Karol Wojtyla, the Pope's given name, speaks numerous languages and almost a billion people come under his direct authority as the head of the Catholic Church. He has also been working feverishly to bring the other world religions under his influence. He has been very successful at this for even Billy Graham extols his virtues.

It seems certain that the False Prophet described in Revelation 13, will arise from the papacy. He is the "beast coming up out of the earth" who will identify the Antichrist as the Messiah and "causeth the earth and them who dwell in it to worship the first beast, whose deadly wound was healed" (Rev. 13:12).

The third Babylon in Scripture has been called Political Babylon, the New Babylon, New Testament Babylon and the Great City Babylon. Scripture gives a detailed and unmistakable description of the Great City Babylon. The Biblical description of the New Babylon is that of a great end-time nation that will be totally destroyed in one hour.

There is no doubt that the United States of America is the great end-time nation so aptly described in Scripture as a nation immensely blessed by God but which turns its back on God just before the return of the Lord Jesus Christ. It is extremely easy to allow one's emotions and biases to cause spiritual blindness when the truth is so painfully close to that which we dearly love. Christians who dearly love America should also remember that their true home is that "...city which hath foundations, whose builder and maker is God" (Heb 11:10).

> Rev 18:4 (KJV)   And I heard another voice from heaven, saying, Come out of her, my people, that ye be not partakers of her sins, and that ye receive not of her plagues.

God's people are in the Great City Babylon and this includes Jews, Christians and some of the Gentiles who will be saved during the tribulation.

God's judgment on New Babylon is described in detail in Jeremiah 50 and 51, and the description of New Babylon is an amazingly detailed and accurate description of America. The time of judgment is when Israel and Judah return to their land (Jer. 50:4-5). This is near the end of the tribulation after all Christians have been raptured. God is urging the Jews to flee Babylon because He is going to stir up a nation from the North. This refers to Russia which is due north of Israel since directions in the Bible are always given in relation to Israel.

Babylon will be destroyed by "arrows" (i.e., Missiles) which will come out of the North (Jer. 51:48). Each one of these "arrows" will hit its mark as if it were shot by a mighty expert (Jer. 50:9). This is a perfect prophetic description of Russia's Intercontinental Ballistic Missiles (ICBM) which have guidance systems and are aimed at America's cities over the North Pole.

A fire will be kindled in the cities of Babylon which will consume everyone around the cities (Jer. 50:32). This accurately describes the aftermath of the detonation of nuclear missiles over American cities. Russia's ICBMs have maintained full fallout lethality to guarantee that people in the cities and around the cities would be killed by the nuclear radiation. Babylon will be totally desolated and the people left in other countries will be astonished and horrified at her plagues. Babylon will not be inhabitable after its destruction (Jer. 50:13). This is clearly because of the nuclear radiation.

The Lord has opened his arsenal and brought out the weapons of His wrath to destroy Babylon completely without even a remnant left (Jer. 50:25-26). God's arsenal contains weapons powered by the atom which is held together by His might. His weapons utilize nuclear energy which is the same energy that powers the sun and all the stars.

The New Babylon is called "O daughter of Babylon" in Jeremiah 50:42. Ancient Babylon did not have a mother since it was founded by Nimrod. Not only does New Babylon have a mother, but she is in existence at the time the New Babylon is destroyed. Also, New Babylon will be a young nation in contrast to the rest of the nations of the world (Jer. 50:12). This is a perfect description of America which is a young nation relative to all other nations, and her mother, Great Britain, is still in existence.

Babylon has been "a golden cup in the Lord's hand" (Jer. 51:7). This means that God has blessed this nation with unprecedented wealth, and it is a nation used by God to accomplish His purpose. However, this nation has turned against God in pride and arrogance. This one verse identifies America as the nation being judged. No other nation has been blessed so abundantly as America and no other nation has changed so dramatically from being God-centered to being man-centered. America has been dramatically used by God in the area of missions, and this was especially true during the Philadelphia Church Age. But the Church has become lukewarm and indifferent in the current Laodicean Church Age.

God "would have healed Babylon" if she would have repented, but she would not be healed (Jer. 51:9). The judgment that befalls Babylon "reaches unto heaven." This is a graphic description of the mushroom clouds that ascend into the heavens after the detonation of the nuclear missiles which destroy Babylon.

Babylon "mounts up to heaven" to fortify her defenses (Jer 51:53). This is a classic description of America's use of satellites in our defense systems. Satellites are useless against the ICBMs though, and verse 53 clearly delineates the futility of these defenses. The knowledge that the missiles are coming does not stop them. America's

Patriot Missiles are not fast enough to catch the Russian ICBMs which travel at 20,000 MPH.

The New Babylon is situated "upon many waters" (Jer. 51:13), and this one verse alone proves that Political Babylon is not Ancient Babylon rebuilt. Of course, the overall description of New Babylon also clearly excludes Ancient Babylon as the nation under judgment at the close of this age.

Chapter 17 of Revelation describes "the great whore that sitteth upon many waters." This harlot is representative of both Ecclesiastical and Political Babylon. Ecclesiastical Babylon, the papal worship system, will be destroyed by the Ten-Horned Beast and its leader, the Antichrist. Chapter 18 of Revelation describes in detail Political Babylon, America, and its sudden catastrophic destruction through the providential act of God. Russia is the instrument used by God to rain down his judgment upon America. The destruction of chapter 17 is a separate event from the destruction of chapter 18 of Revelation.

New Babylon has "become the habitation of devils, and the hold of every foul spirit, and a cage of every unclean and hateful bird" (Rev. 18:2). This clearly enunciates how patently evil America has become. Birds in Scripture represent evil and the growth of evil. In America, adultery, fornication, drunkenness, drug use, abortion, arrogance, murder, homosexuality, gluttony, gossip, covetousness, materialism and numerous other demonstrations of outright wickedness have become so commonplace that even Christians have become desensitized to them. America has gone past the point of no return in its wickedness and is now being ripened for God's judgment. Of course, the Antichrist will first be given his authority for 42 months, and God's people will be removed before the judgments of God will be rained down.

"For all the nations have drunk the wine of the wrath of her fornication" (Rev. 18:3). America is the only nation that has fulfilled this prophecy completely. It is common knowledge that American popular culture is overrunning the world. The phenomenon is called "the Americanization of the world," and even secular figures from the world of scholarship, entertainment and communications do not believe it is good.

The export of America's music, movies and television is spreading the dark, self-indulgent side of American civilization throughout the world. Pop culture is not only trashing America's values but that of the entire world. This spread of American pop culture has been credited with the fall of communism, but it teaches a hedonistic and destructive lifestyle that debases the audiences that receive it. God's assessment is accurate.

"The merchants of the earth are waxed rich through the abundance of her delicacies" (Rev. 18:3). This is a concise and amazingly accurate description of America's infatuation with the god of materialism. America has become a nation drunk with the desire for more and more possessions and wealth. Americans are no longer content to have reliable means of transportation. That transportation must now be a Mercedes, Lexus, BMW, Ferrari or some other vehicle whose primary function is to impress friends and neighbors. Even Christians are drunk with these desires and will have to account for their use of the wealth that they have received. This accountability will take place at the Judgment Seat of Christ.

America will receive as much torture and grief as the glory and luxury she gave herself (Rev. 18:7). She boasts as a "Queen" who "shall see no sorrow." America sees herself as being invincible, and this arrogant attitude is a sure sign of a coming fall.

> Rev 18:2 (KJV) And he cried mightily with a strong voice, saying, Babylon the great is fallen, is fallen...

The diadem worn by the Statue of Liberty is identical to the one worn by Ishtar, the ancient Babylonian goddess of love and war. It is also highly significant that New York City, the city that represents America to the world, is called "Babylon on the Hudson." The idea that political Babylon will be a rebuilt city in Iraq is a futile attempt at escaping reality and a determined attempt to delay the coming of the Lord Jesus Christ. The Biblical description of the New Babylon is such a perfect and comprehensive description of America that it is difficult to understand why all Christians cannot see this. It has become clear that this blindness is motivated by self-deception rather than a lack of Biblical evidence.

The clincher for the identification of America as the New Babylon is in Revelation 18:16. This Scripture describes Babylon the Great as being clothed in red, white and blue. The word for "blue" is translated as "purple", but no Greek word is translated "blue" in the New Testament, and the corresponding Hebrew word in the Old Testament is translated "blue".

All cargoes imported and exported by Babylon the Great are listed in Revelation 18:11-13, and all of these cargoes are imports or exports of America. They have caused the world's ship owners to become wealthy (Rev. 18:19). Of key importance is the trafficking in "bodies and souls of men" (Rev. 18:13). This is a reference to America's purchase of African slaves prior to the Civil War.

Babylon the Great will be totally destroyed in one day when she will be consumed by fire as the Lord God judges her (Rev. 18:8). Three times the Scriptures state that her doom will come in "one hour" (Rev. 18:10,17,19). It is not a coincidence that one hour is the time estimated for Russia's missiles to be fired and detonate over our cities. They are aimed at us over the North Pole and they take about 20 minutes to reach their destination.

One final prophecy about Babylon is that she will be caught in "a snare" (Jer 50:24). She "wast not aware," and she will be totally annihilated. Babylon lowered her guard. This is exactly what is happening right now in America. We are unilaterally disarming by dismantling nuclear weapons and decreasing defense spending. America has been tricked into complacency by Russia's collapse and overtures for peace. Russia has not dismantled one nuclear missile and has no intention of doing so.

The above prophecies about Babylon the Great are only a smattering of the prophecies in Scripture that give a detailed description of her. They are representative and should provide the reader with a clear picture of America's part in the prophetic puzzle. This means doomsday for America and those who have never placed their faith and trust in Jesus Christ. It is not a doomsday scenario for believers since God's people will be removed before His wrath is released upon the earth.

God judged the earth with a flood, and He judged Sodom and Gomorrah with fire and brimstone. America will surely be judged for its sins.

Before the destruction of America, the "man of sin" must be revealed. He is the Antichrist, "the beast that was, and is not, and yet is" (Rev. 17:8).

The book of Revelation describes a great harlot seen riding on Daniel's beast with seven heads and ten horns (Revelation 17:1-3). The Apostle John describes this great harlot as the "beast out of the earth" (Revelation 13), also known as the false prophet.

The above pictures are provided courtesy of Pastor Randy Shupe, whose books may be found in the Bibliography on page 38.

Appendix 5 is a copy of Chapter 9 of *The Open Door*, by Lyn Mize, courtesy of his family. Copyright © 2022, LYN MiZE, EST.

Appendix 6 – Signs of Christ's Coming

Many modern Bible teachers and students believe that the rebirth of the nation of Israel represents the budding of the *fig tree* that Jesus described to His disciples as He sat on the Mount of Olives, and we are living in the generation that won't pass away before He returns.

> *Verily I say unto you, this generation shall not pass,*
> *till all these things be fulfilled.* (Matthew 24:34 – KJV)

With Israel becoming a nation in 1948, we have been alerted that the Lord's return is fast approaching. Jesus also told his disciples a second sign to look for in the parable of Noah:

> *As it was in the days of Noah,*
> *so it will be at the coming of the Son of Man.*
> (Matthew 24:37 – NIV)

Here the Lord is telling the Church that just before His return, things will be the same as they were back in Noah's day. This pictures life going on right up until the day that the rapture occurs, and the judgments of God are suddenly released upon the earth. A careful study of Genesis 6 will alert the reader to the fact that living in these end times is almost parallel to the time before the flood. The world has become a great cesspool of corruption, violence, sex, drugs, idolatry, witchcraft and other perversions. Reading the account in Genesis is like reading today's newspaper or listening to the daily news.

In the Lord's parable concerning Noah, Jesus was also giving us a second important sign that His return is drawing very near. Several years ago a famous comet passed through our solar system and it was hailed as the most-watched comet of all time.

April 8, 1997

Comet Hale-Bopp Over New York City
Credit and Copyright: J. Sivo
http://antwrp.gsfc.nasa.gov/apod/ap970408.html
"What's that point of light above the World Trade Center? It's Comet Hale-Bopp! Both faster than a speeding bullet and able to "leap" tall buildings in its single <u>orbit</u>, Comet Hale-Bopp is also bright enough to be seen even over the glowing lights of one of the world's premier cities. In the foreground lies the East River, while much of New York City's Lower Manhattan can be seen between the river and the comet."

As it was in the days of Noah,
so it will be at the coming of the Son of Man.
(Matthew 24:37 – NIV)

These words from our wonderful Lord have several applications about the Tribulation period that is about to ensnare this world.

Seas Lifted Up

Throughout the Old Testament, the time of the coming Tribulation period is described as the time when the "seas have lifted up," and also as coming in as a "flood" (please see Jeremiah 51:42, Hosea 5:10, Daniel 11:40 and Psalm 93:3-4 for just a few examples).

This is a direct parallel to the time of Noah when the Great Flood of water came to wipe out every living creature except for righteous Noah and his family, and the pairs of animals God spared. While God said He would never flood the earth again with water, the coming Judgement will be by fire (II Peter 3:10). The book of Revelation shows that approximately three billion people will perish in the terrible time that lies ahead (see Revelation 6:8 and 9:15).

2 Witnesses

A guiding principle of God is to establish a matter based upon the witness of two or more:

> ...*a matter must be established by the testimony of two or three witnesses* (Deuteronomy 19:15 – NIV)

In 1994, God was able to get the attention of mankind when Comet Shoemaker-Levy crashed into Jupiter on the 9th of Av (on the Jewish calendar). Interestingly, this Comet was named after the "two" witnesses who first discovered it.

In 1995, "two" more astronomers also discovered another comet. It was called Comet Hale-Bopp, and it reached its closest approach to planet Earth on March 23, 1997. It has been labeled as the most widely viewed comet in the history of mankind.

Scientists have determined that Comet Hale-Bopp's orbit brought it to our solar system 4,465 years ago (see Notes 1 and 2 below). In other words, the comet made its appearance near Earth in 1997 and also in 2468 BC. Remarkably, this comet preceded the Great Flood by 120 years! God warned Noah of this in Genesis 6:3:

> *My Spirit shall not strive with man forever, for he is indeed flesh; yet his days shall be one hundred and twenty years.*

Days of Noah

What does all of this have to do with the Lord's return? Noah was born around 2948 BC, and Genesis 7:11 tells us that the Flood took place when Noah was 600, or in 2348 BC.

Remember, our Lord told us: ***"As it was in the days of Noah, so it will be at the coming of the Son of Man.***
(Matthew 24:37 – NIV)

In the original Greek, it is saying: ***"exactly like"*** it was, so it will be when He comes (see Strong's #5618).

During the days of Noah, Comet Hale-Bopp arrived on the scene as a harbinger of the Great Flood. Just as this same comet appeared before the Flood, could its arrival again in 1997 be a sign that God's final Judgement, also known as the time of Jacob's Trouble, is about to begin?

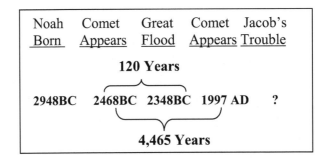

Comet Hale-Bopp arrived 120 years before the Flood as a warning to mankind. Only righteous Noah heeded God's warning and built the ark, as God instructed. By faith, Noah was obedient to God and, as a result, saved himself and his family from destruction.

Remember, Jesus told us His return would be preceded by great heavenly signs: *"And there shall be signs in the sun, and in the moon, and in the stars; and upon the earth distress of nations, with perplexity; the sea and the waves roaring..."* (Luke 21:25)

> Jesus was asked 3 questions by the disciples:
> *"Tell us, (1) when shall these things be"* (the destruction of *the city of Jerusalem), " and (2) what shall be the **sign** of thy coming, and (3) of the end of the world?"* (Matthew 24:3)

Just as this large comet appeared as a 120-year warning to Noah, its arrival in 1997 tells us that Jesus is getting ready to return again. Is this the **"Sign"** Jesus referred to?

Sign of Christ's Coming

The **first** question had to do with events that were fulfilled in 70 AD. The **third** question has to do with the future time at the very end of the age.

The **second** question, however, has to do with the time of Christ's second coming.   Jesus answered this second question in His description of the days of Noah found in Matthew 24:33-39:

> [37] **But as the days of Noe were, so shall also the coming of the Son of man be.** [38] *For as in the days that were before the flood they were eating and drinking, marrying and giving in marriage, until the day that Noe entered into the ark,* [39] *And knew not until the flood came, and took them all away; so shall also the coming of the Son of man be.*

Jesus is telling us that the **_sign_** of His coming will be as it was during the days of Noah.   As Comet Hale-Bopp was a sign to the people in Noah's day, its arrival in 1997 is a sign that Jesus is coming back again soon.   Comet Hale-Bopp could be the very sign Jesus was referring to, which would announce His return for His faithful.

Remember, Jesus said, *"**exactly as** it was in the days of Noah, so will it be when He returns."*   The appearance of Comet Hale-Bopp in 1997 is a strong indication that the Tribulation period is about to begin, but before then, Jesus is coming for His bride!

Keep looking up! Jesus is coming again very soon!
As Noah prepared for the destruction God warned him about 120 years before the Flood, Jesus has given mankind a final warning that the Tribulation period is about to begin.   The horrible destruction on 9/11 is only a precursor of what is about to take place on planet Earth.   We need to be wise like Noah and prepare.   Always remember our Lord's instructions in Luke 21:34-36:

> *(34)And take heed to yourselves, lest at any time your hearts be overcharged with surfeiting, and drunkenness, and cares of this life, and so that day come upon you unawares. (35) For as a snare shall it come on all them that dwell on the face of the whole earth.*
> *(36)**Watch ye therefore, and _pray always_, that ye may be accounted worthy to escape all these things that shall come to pass, and to stand before the Son of man** (Luke 21:34-36).*

Footnotes to Appendix 6

(1) The original orbit of Comet Hale-Bopp was calculated to be approximately 265 years by engineer George Sanctuary in his article, *Three Craters In Israel*, published on 3/31/01 found in the Supplemental Articles for *Coming Spiritual Earthquake*.

Comet Hale-Bopp's orbit around the time of the Flood changed from 265 years to about 4,200 years. Because the plane of the comet's orbit is perpendicular to the earth's orbital plane (ecliptic), Mr. Sanctuary noted: "A negative time increment was used for this simulation...to back the comet away from the earth.... past Jupiter... and then out of the solar system. The simulation suggests that the past-past orbit had a very eccentric orbit with a period of only 265 years. When the comet passed Jupiter (*around 2203BC*) its orbit was deflected upward, coming down near the earth 15 months later with the comet's period changed from 265 years to about (*4,200*) years." (*added text for clarity*)

(2) Don Yeomans, with NASA's Jet Propulsion Laboratory, made the following observations regarding the comet's orbit: "By integrating the above orbit forward and backward in time until the comet leaves the planetary system and then referring the osculating orbital elements...the following orbital periods result: Original orbital period before entering planetary system = 4200 years. Future orbital period after exiting the planetary system = 2380 years."

This analysis can be found at:

http://www2.jpl.nasa.gov/comet/ephemjpl6.html

Based upon the above two calculations we have the following:

265 [a] + 4,200 [b] = 4,465 Years

1997 AD – 4,465 Years = 2468 BC = Hale Bopp arrived

(a) Orbit period calculated by George Sanctuary before deflection around 2203 BC.

(b) Orbit period calculated by Don Yeomans after 1997 visit.

Tract Included In Appendix 6

This tract was written in 1997 when Comet Hale-Bopp entered our solar system. In 2027 it will be the 30th Anniversary of its last appearance. Bullinger wrote, "30, being 3x10 denotes in a higher degree the perfection of Divine order, as marking the **right moment**. Christ was thirty years of age at the commencement of His ministry. David was also 30 when he began to reign." (Bullinger, p. 265). Was Comet Hale-Bopp giving us a sign that the bride of Christ is about to begin her reign and Christ will return in 2027? **Is this further corroboration that 2027 will be the time for Christ's Second Coming?** (See Ezekiel 33:1-6).

Special Invitation

This booklet was primarily written for those who have been born again. If you have never been born again, would you like to be? The Bible shows that it's simple to be saved…

- **Realize you are a sinner.**
  "As it is written, There is none righteous, no, not one:"
  (Romans 3:10)
  "… for there is no difference. For all have sinned, and come short of the glory of God;" (Romans 3:22-23)

- **Realize you CAN NOT save yourself.**
  "But we are all as an unclean thing, and all our righteousness are as filthy rags; …" (Isaiah 64:6)
  "Not by works of righteousness which we have done, but according to his mercy he saved us, …" (Titus 3:5)

- **Realize that Jesus Christ died on the cross to pay for your sins.**
  "Who his own self bare our sins in his own body on the tree,…"
  (I Peter 2:24)
  "… Unto him that loved us, and washed us from our sins in his own blood," (Revelation 1:5)

- **Simply by faith receive Jesus Christ as your personal Savior.**
  "But as many as received him, to them gave he power to become the sons of God, even to them that believe on his name:" (John 1:12)
  " …Sirs, what must I do to be saved? And they said, Believe on the Lord Jesus Christ, and thou shalt be saved, and thy house."
  (Acts 16:30-31)

WOULD YOU LIKE TO BE SAVED?

If you would like to be saved, believe on the Lord Jesus Christ right now by making this acknowledgment in your heart:

> Lord Jesus, I know that I am a sinner, and unless You save me, I am lost forever. I thank You for dying for me at Calvary. By faith I come to You now, Lord, the best way I know how, and ask You to save me. I believe that God raised You from the dead and acknowledge You as my personal Saviour.

If you believed on the Lord, this is the most important decision of your life. You are now saved by the precious blood of Jesus Christ, which was shed for you and your sins. Now that you have believed on Jesus as your personal Saviour, you will want to find a Church where you can be baptized as your first act of obedience, and where the Word of God is taught so you can continue to grow in your faith. Ask the Holy Spirit to help you as you read the Bible to learn all that God has for your life.

Also, please see the Bibliography, as well as the pages that follow for information on several books that will help you on your wonderful journey and help you prepare for the days ahead.

Endtimes
The Bible indicates that we are living in the final days and Jesus Christ is getting ready to return very soon. This book was written to help Christians prepare for what lies ahead. The Word of God indicates that the Tribulation Period is rapidly approaching and that the Antichrist is getting ready to emerge on the world scene.

Jesus promised His disciples that there is a way to escape the horrible time of testing and persecution that will soon devastate this planet. The main purpose of this book is to help you get prepared so you will rule and reign with Jesus when He returns.

About The Author

Jim Harman has been a Christian for more than 45 years. He has diligently studied the Word of God with a particular emphasis on Prophecy. Jim has written several books and the most essential titles are available at www.ProphecyCountdown.com: ***The Coming Spiritual Earthquake, The Kingdom, Overcomers' Guide To The Kingdom, Calling All Overcomers, Come Away My Beloved, Daniel's Prophecies Unsealed, and Salvation of the Soul;*** which have been widely distributed around the world. These books will encourage you to continue *"Looking"* for the Lord's soon return.

Jim's professional experience included being a Certified Public Accountant (CPA) and a Certified Property Manager (CPM). He had an extensive background in both public accounting and financial management with several well-known national firms.

Jim was fortunate to have been acquainted with several mature believers who understand and teach the deeper truths of the Bible. It is Jim's strong desire that many will come to realize the vital importance of seeking the Kingdom and seeking Christ's righteousness as we approach the soon return of our Lord and Saviour Jesus Christ.

The burden of Jim's heart is to see many believers come to know the joy of Christ's triumph in their lives as they become true overcomers; qualified and ready to rule and reign with Christ in the coming Kingdom.

To contact Jim for questions, to arrange for speaking engagements, or to order multiple copies of his books:

Jim Harman
P.O. Box 941612
Maitland, FL 32794
JimHarmanCPA@gmail.com

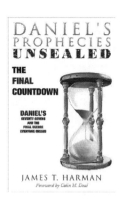

Join best-selling author James Harman as he explores the shocking new evidence of how President Donald Trump initiated the final peace initiative alluded to by the prophet Daniel. His Peace to Prosperity Plan along with the Abraham Accords began the Final Countdown.

This timely book reveals how the Temple Mount will soon take center stage when the Antichrist ushers in the time Jesus described as Great Tribulation. Jesus provides a way of escape for those believers who are ready. The purpose of this book is to help you prepare to escape a time that Jesus said would be like no other time in all of human history.

The Final Countdown is a sequel to the Top-10 Best-Selling *Daniel's Prophecies Unsealed*. Thanks to the incredible discovery by Dr. Christian Widener, the book of Daniel has been unsealed. James Harman has summarized this important message to help prepare the end-time Church for the days ahead. Daniel was told that the words would be closed up and sealed until the time of the end. Dr. Widener's finding is truly a treasured gem you don't want to miss.

Now is the time to prepare and help others prepare before the time of the Great Tribulation arrives. Jesus provides a way of escape for those blameless believers who are ready. The purpose of this book is to help you prepare.

Order your copy today *Paperback – eBook – Audio* Editions

The Open Door was written to reveal the Scriptures that will help you learn how to watch for, and be a part of Jesus Christ's coming Kingdom. If you are seeking more than simple answers, this book will show you the deeper truths in the Scriptures that will lead you to a closeness with Christ now, and a position with Him in His coming Kingdom in the very near future.

The message in this timely prophetic book will help you understand:

- The Judgment Seat Christ will not be an award ceremony for every Christian.
- Which one of the Seven Feasts the Rapture will occur on.
- How you can obtain the 5 Crowns mentioned in the Bible.
- How you can ensure you will be part of the Bride of Christ.
- What the Seven Parables of the Kingdom really mean.
- Which of the Seven Churches you should be a member in.
- The future destiny of the United States of America.
- The startling identity of the Antichrist who is about to emerge.
- How you can escape the coming tribulation period.
- How you can reign and rule with the King of the Universe.

Jesus went away almost 2,000 years ago and He is in the process of preparing a Holy City for all overcoming believers. Lyn Mize has given us an excellent resource that can be instrumental in helping us qualify to become part of those who will reign and rule with Jesus in this magnificent Holy City.

Available From Amazon.com

Paperback, **Kindle** and **Audible** Editions

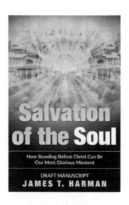

HOW STANDING BEFORE CHRIST
CAN BE OUR MOST GLORIOUS MOMENT

The topic of the Judgment Seat of Christ is often neglected by today's modern church.

> *"For we must all appear before the judgment seat of Christ, that each one may receive the things done in the body, according to what he has done, whether good or bad"* (2 Corinthians 5:10).

When Jesus returns, He will review all of our lives to determine whether we have been faithful and obedient doers of His Word. The purpose of this book is to prepare believers so they will be able to hear Him say:

> *"Well done, good and faithful servant....*
> ***Enter into the joy of your lord"*** (Matthew 25:21).

MUST-READ FOR ALL BELIEVERS

NEW DISCOVERY – LEARN ABOUT
- Difference between the salvation of spirit and soul.
- What Jesus meant by *"take up your cross."*
- How the Word of God can save our souls.
- When the salvation of our soul takes place.
- Sign of Christ's Coming

Download your FREE copy: www.ProphecyCountdown.com

Order your copy today ***Paperback – eBook – Audio*** Editions

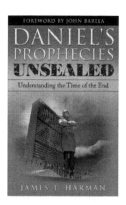

"Go your way Daniel, because the words are closed up and sealed until the time of the end...none of the wicked will understand, but those who are wise will understand."
(Daniel 12:9-10)

The Archangel Michael told Daniel that the prophecies would be sealed until the time of the end. Discover how the prophecies in the book of Daniel are being unsealed in the events taking place today.

Since Daniel was told that the wise will understand the message and lead many to righteousness, while the wicked will not grasp its meaning and will continue in their wickedness, it is imperative for everyone living in these end times to diligently examine and attempt to comprehend the vital message Daniel has recorded for us. The wise will diligently search the word of the Lord and ask for wisdom in order to understand God's plan.

When Jesus came the first time, the wise men of the day were aware of His soon arrival and they were actively looking for Him. Today, those who are wise will be passionately sharing this message and helping others prepare. Those doing so will *"shine like the stars forever and ever."*

May the Lord grant us a heart of wisdom to understand the time we are living in so we can prepare for what lies ahead!

Download your FREE copy: www.ProphecyCountdown.com

Order your copy today: ***Paperback – eBook – Audio*** Editions

God placed the *Song of Solomon* in the heart of the Bible for a special reason. *Come Away My Beloved* helps reveal that reason in a most enchanting way. In this refreshing commentary, you will realize why this ancient love story has perplexed Bible students and commentators down through the ages.

Find out the prophetic importance veiled within the Song's poetic imagery and experience a renewed love for the Lord as you explore one of the most passionate love stories of all time.

Witness the wonderful joys of romance and devotion shared by two young lovers. Discover enduring lessons of virtue and faithfulness, and learn amazing truths that have been hidden within the greatest love Song ever written.

Written almost 3,000 years ago this brilliant Song of love reflects God's desire for every man and woman; not only in their present lives but also in their relationship with Him.

This book will revive your heart with a fervent love for your Saviour. It will also help you prepare for your glorious wedding day when Jesus returns for His devoted bride.

Allow this beautiful story of love and passion to ignite a flame in your heart and let this inspirational Song arouse your heart to join in the impassioned cry with the rest of the bride:

"Make haste, my beloved, and come quickly…"
Download your FREE copy: www.ProphecyCountdown.com

Order your copy today: *Paperback – eBook* Editions

Perplexed by the book of Revelation? Not sure what all the signs, symbols and metaphors really mean? Jim Harman's latest work unravels Apostle John's remarkable revelation of Jesus Christ and what's in store for the inhabitants of planet Earth. This extraordinary commentary is not another cookie-cutter rehash of the popular teachings fostered by the *Left Behind* phenomena so prevalent in today's church.

One of the central messages in the book of Revelation is that God is calling men to be genuine overcomers. Jesus Christ has been sent out from the throne of God to conquer men's hearts so they can also be overcomers.

The purpose of this book is to encourage people to embrace Him as the King of their hearts and allow His life to reign in theirs. He wants you to be able to overcome by His mighty power and strength living inside of you just as He overcame for all of us. Jesus will be looking for a faithful remnant qualified to rule and reign with Him when He returns. This book will help you prepare to be the overcomer for which Jesus is looking.

The reader will come away with a new and enlightened understanding of what the last book in God's Word is all about. Understand the book of Revelation and why it is so important for believers living in the last days of the Church age.

Download your FREE copy: www.ProphecyCountdown.com

Order your copy today: *Paperback – eBook* Editions

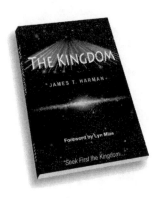

Once a person is saved, the number one priority should be seeking entrance into the Kingdom through the salvation of their soul. It is pictured as a runner in a race seeking a prize represented by a crown that will last forever.

The salvation of the soul and entrance into the coming Kingdom are only achieved through much testing and the trial of one's faith. If you are going through difficulty, then REJOICE:

> *"Blessed is the man who perseveres under trial, because when he has stood the test, he will receive the crown of life that God has promised to those who love Him."* (James 1:12)

The "Traditional" teaching on the "THE KINGDOM" has taken the Church captive into believing all Christians will rule and reign with Christ no matter if they have lived faithful and obedient lives, or if they have been slothful and disobedient with the talents God has given them. Find out the important Truth before Jesus Christ returns.

MUST READING FOR EVERY CHRISTIAN

Jesus Christ is returning for His faithful overcoming followers. Don't miss the opportunity of ruling and reigning with Christ in the coming KINGDOM!

Download your FREE copy: www.ProphecyCountdown.com

Order your copy today: ***Paperback – eBook*** Editions

Get ready to climb back up the Mountain to listen to Christ's teachings once again. Though you may have read His great **Sermon on the Mount** many times, discover exciting promises that many have missed.

The purpose of this book is to help Christians be the Overcomers Jesus wants them to be and to help them gain their own entrance in the coming Kingdom. Learn what seeking the Kingdom of God is all about and be among the chosen few who will "enter into" the coming Kingdom. *"Whoever hears these sayings of Mine, and does them, I will liken him to a wise man who built his house upon the rock."* (Matthew 7:24)

Also, learn about:
- The link between Beatitudes and Fruit of the Spirit
- What the "law of Christ" really is
- The critical importance of the "Lord's prayer"
- How to be an Overcomer
- THE SIGN of Christ's soon Coming
- A new song entitled: LOOKING FOR THE SON which has the message of how vitally important it is to be Watching for the Lord's return and the consequences to those who are not looking.

Download your FREE copy: www.ProphecyCountdown.com

Order your copy today: *Paperback – eBook – Audio* Editions

CHRISTIAN WIDENER

WITNESSING THE END

For Born-Again Believers
Looking For The Return Of Their
Lord and Savior Jesus Christ

*Learn How A Decree From 1537 AD
Is About To Change Your Life.*

Regardless Of What You Know About Bible Prophecy, This Book <u>Will</u> Shock You…

Clear Answers to Important Prophetic Questions

- ✓ What does the age of the earth mean for the timing of the return of Christ?
- ✓ Is the cycle of Jubilee years actually revealed in Scripture?
- ✓ Have there really been prophecies being fulfilled right under most people's noses?
- ✓ What can I do to prepare and be ready?

After 2000 Years, Jesus Christ's Return is Finally Approaching

This is a timely & special adventure filled with meticulously researched evidence that you don't want to miss!

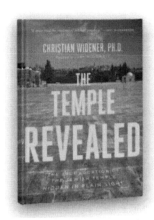

★★★★★
Everyone Interested
In The Temple Mount Needs To Take This
Study Seriously.

★★★★★
Wow! This Really
Is Excellent Work.
I Think You Have
Me Convinced,
Honestly.

★★★★★
Both Biblical And
Logical

GET YOUR COPY TODAY!

CHRISTIAN WIDENER

THE TEMPLE REVEALED

For Truth Seeking Dot-Connectors, Looking To Solve An Ancient Mystery

Learn How An Engineers Crumbling Faith In The Scholars Was Used To
Uncover The "Prophetic" Secret To Unraveling 3,000 Years Of Temple Mount History,
By Exposing Two Hidden Landmarks…

Easy To Follow With Clear Photos
- ✓ The "living waters" mistake you don't know you're making
- ✓ Where to build the new temple without disturbing the "Dome of the rock"
- ✓ Why biased researchers just won't change their minds
- ✓ What all doubters should know about the exposed bedrock
- ✓ How we know the Golden Gate is a true landmark from the temple

Rethink Your Interpretation
- ✓ Basic mistakes even smart researchers make
- ✓ Don't believe what you've been told about the Gihon Springs
- ✓ Where evidence for the first Temple is and how to get it
- ✓ For people who want to learn about the Temple but don't know where to get started

LOOKING FOR THE SON
Lyrics by Jim Harman
Listen to this Song on the Home Page of Prophecy Countdown

Lyric	Scripture
There's a fire burning in my heart	Luke 24:32
Yearning for the Lord to come,	Rev. 22:17, Mat. 6:33
and His Kingdom come to start	
Soon He'll come.....so enter the narrow gate	Lk. 21:34-36, Mat.7:13
Even though you mock me now...	II Peter 3:4
He'll come to set things straight	
Watch how I'll leave in the twinkling of an eye	I Corinthians 15:52
Don't be surprised when I go up in the sky	Revelation 3:10
There's a fire burning in my heart	Luke 24:32
Yearning for my precious Lord	Revelation 22:17
And His Kingdom come to start	Revelation 20:4-6
Your love of this world, has forsaken His	I John 2:15
It leaves me knowing that you could have had it all	Revelation 21:7
Your love of this world, was oh so reckless	Revelation 3:14-22
I can't help thinking	Philippians 1:3-6
You would have had it all	Revelation 21:7
Looking for the Son	Titus 2:13, Luke 21:36
(Tears are gonna fall, not looking for the Son)	Matthew 25:10-13
You had His holy Word in your hand	II Timothy 3:16
(You're gonna wish you had listened to me)	Jeremiah 25:4-8
And you missed it...for your self	Matthew 22:11-14
(Tears are gonna fall, not looking for the Son)	Matthew 25:10-13
Brother, I have a story to be told	Habakkuk 2:2
It's the only one that's true	John 3:16-17
And it should've made your heart turn	II Peter 3:9
Remember me when I rise up in the air	I Corinthians 15:52
Leaving your home down here	I Corinthians 15:52
For true Treasures beyond compare	Matthew 6:20
Your love of this world, has forsaken His	I John 2:15
It leaves me knowing that you could have had it all	Revelation 21:7
Your love of this world, was oh so reckless	Revelation 3:14-22
I can't help thinking	Philippians 1:3-6
You would have had it all	Revelation 21:7

(Lyrics in parentheses represent background vocals)

(CONTINUED)

Lyric	Scripture
Looking for the Son	Titus 2:13, Lk. 21:36
(Tears are gonna fall, not looking for the Son)	Matthew 25:10-13
You had His holy Word in your hand	II Timothy 3:16
(You're gonna wish you had listened to me)	Jeremiah 25:4-8
And you lost it...for your self	Matthew 22:11-14
(Tears are gonna fall, not looking for the Son)	Matthew 25:10-13
You would have had it all	Revelation 21:7
Looking for the Son	Titus 2:13, Lk. 21:36
You had His holy Word in your hand	II Timothy 3:16
But you missed it... for your self	Matthew 22:11-14
Lov'n the world....not the open door	I Jn. 2:15, Rev. 4:1
Down the broad way... blind to what life's really for	Matthew 7:13-14
Turn around now...while there still is time	I Jn. 1:9, II Pet. 3:9
Learn your lesson now or you'll reap just what you sow	Galatians 6:7

(You're gonna wish you had listened to me)
You would have had it all
(Tears are gonna fall, not looking for the Son)
You would have had it all
(You're gonna wish you had listened to me)
It all, it all, it all
(Tears are gonna fall, not looking for the Son)

You would have had it all
(You're gonna wish you had listened to me)
Looking for the Son
(Tears are gonna fall, not looking for the Son)
You had His holy Word in your hand
(You're gonna wish you had listened to me)
And you missed it...for yourself
(Tears are gonna fall, not looking for the Son)

You would have had it all
(You're gonna wish you had listened to me)
Looking for the Son
(Tears are gonna fall, not looking for the Son)
You had His holy Word in your hand
(You're gonna wish you had listened to me)
But you missed it
You missed it
You missed it
You missed it....for yourself

Scripture Summary
Jeremiah 25:4-8
Habakkuk 2:2
Matthew 6:20
Matthew 6:33
Matthew 7:13
Matthew 22:11-14
Matthew 25:10-13
Luke 21:34-36
Luke 24:332
John 3:16-17
I Corinthians 15:52
Galatians 6:7
Philippians 1:3-6
II Timothy 3:16
Titus 2:13
II Peter 3:9
II Peter 3:4
I John 1:9
I John 2:15
Revelation 3:10
Revelation 3:14-22
Revelation 4:1
Revelation 20:4-6
Revelation 21:7
Revelation 22:17

(See www.ProphecyCountdown.com for more information)

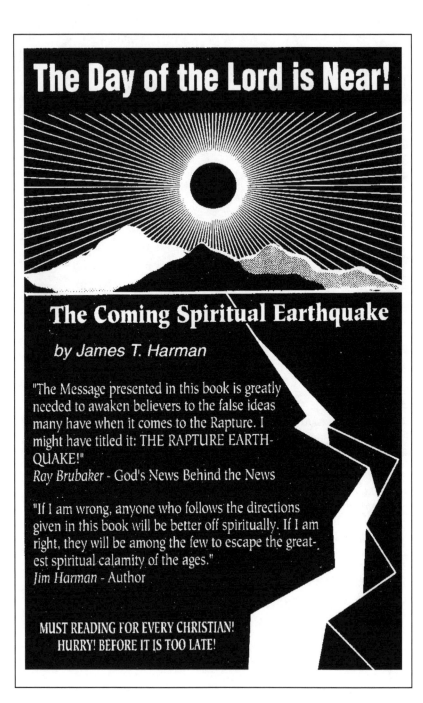

The Day of the Lord is Near!

The Coming Spiritual Earthquake

by James T. Harman

"The Message presented in this book is greatly needed to awaken believers to the false ideas many have when it comes to the Rapture. I might have titled it: THE RAPTURE EARTHQUAKE!"
Ray Brubaker - God's News Behind the News

"If I am wrong, anyone who follows the directions given in this book will be better off spiritually. If I am right, they will be among the few to escape the greatest spiritual calamity of the ages."
Jim Harman - Author

**MUST READING FOR EVERY CHRISTIAN!
HURRY! BEFORE IT IS TOO LATE!**

Made in the USA
Middletown, DE
20 August 2024

59531704R00051